ANDERSON'S
Law School Publications

Administrative Law Anthology
Thomas O. Sargentich

Administrative Law: Cases and Materials
Daniel J. Gifford

Alternative Dispute Resolution: Strategies for Law and Business
E. Wendy Trachte-Huber and Stephen K. Huber

American Legal Systems: A Resource and Reference Guide
Toni M. Fine

An Admiralty Law Anthology
Robert M. Jarvis

Analytic Jurisprudence Anthology
Anthony D'Amato

An Antitrust Anthology
Andrew I. Gavil

Appellate Advocacy: Principles and Practice: Cases and Materials, Second Edition
Ursula Bentele and Eve Cary

Basic Accounting Principles for Lawyers: With Present Value and Expected Value
C. Steven Bradford and Gary A. Ames

A Capital Punishment Anthology (and Electronic Caselaw Appendix)
Victor L. Streib

Cases and Problems in Criminal Law, Third Edition
Myron Moskovitz

The Citation Workbook
Maria L. Ciampi, Rivka Widerman, and Vicki Lutz

Civil Procedure: Cases, Materials, and Questions
Richard D. Freer and Wendy C. Perdue

Clinical Anthology: Readings for Live-Client Clinics
Alex J. Hurder, Frank S. Bloch, Susan L. Brooks, and Susan L. Kay

Commercial Transactions: Problems and Materials
Louis F. Del Duca, Egon Guttman, Alphonse M. Squillante, Fred H. Miller, and Peter Winship
    Vol. 1: Secured Transactions Under the UCC
    Vol. 2: Sales Under the UCC and the CISG
    Vol. 3: Negotiable Instruments Under the UCC and the CIBN

Communications Law: Media, Entertainment, and Regulation
Donald E. Lively, Allen S. Hammond, IV, Blake D. Morant, and Russell L. Weaver

A Conflict-of-Laws Anthology
Gene R. Shreve

A Constitutional Law Anthology
Michael J. Glennon

Constitutional Conflicts, Part I
Derrick A. Bell, Jr.

Constitutional Law: Cases, History, and Dialogues
Donald E. Lively, Phoebe A. Haddon, Dorothy E. Roberts, and Russell L. Weaver

The Constitutional Law of the European Union
James D. Dinnage and John F. Murphy

The Constitutional Law of the European Union: Documentary Supplement
James D. Dinnage and John F. Murphy

Constitutional Torts
Sheldon H. Nahmod, Michael L. Wells, and Thomas A. Eaton

Contracts
Contemporary Cases, Comments, and Problems
Michael L. Closen, Richard M. Perlmutter, and Jeffrey D. Wittenberg

A Contracts Anthology, Second Edition
Peter Linzer

A Corporate Law Anthology
Franklin A. Gevurtz

Corporate and White Collar Crime: An Anthology
Leonard Orland

A Criminal Law Anthology
Arnold H. Loewy

Criminal Law: Cases and Materials
Arnold H. Loewy

A Criminal Procedure Anthology
Silas J. Wasserstrom and Christie L. Snyder

Criminal Procedure: Arrest and Investigation
Arnold H. Loewy and Arthur B. LaFrance

Criminal Procedure: Trial and Sentencing
Arthur B. LaFrance and Arnold H. Loewy

Economic Regulation: Cases and Materials
Richard J. Pierce, Jr.

Elements of Law
Eva H. Hanks, Michael E. Herz, and Steven S. Nemerson

Ending It: Dispute Resolution in America
Descriptions, Examples, Cases and Questions
Susan M. Leeson and Bryan M. Johnston

Environmental Law, Second Edition
Jackson B. Battle, Robert L. Fischman, Maxine I. Lipeles, and Mark S. Squillace
    Vol. 1: Environmental Decisionmaking: NEPA and the Endangered Species Act
    Vol. 2: Water Pollution
    Vol. 3: Air Pollution
    Vol. 4: Hazardous Waste

An Environmental Law Anthology
Robert L. Fischman, Maxine I. Lipeles, and Mark S. Squillace

Environmental Protection and Justice
Readings and Commentary on Environmental Law and Practice
Kenneth A. Manaster

An Evidence Anthology
Edward J. Imwinkelried and Glen Weissenberger

Federal Evidence Courtroom Manual
Glen Weissenberger

Federal Income Tax Anthology
Paul L. Caron, Karen C. Burke, and Grayson M.P. McCouch

Federal Rules of Evidence, 1996-97 Edition
Rules, Legislative History, Commentary and Authority
Glen Weissenberger

Federal Rules of Evidence Handbook, 1996-97 Edition
Publisher's Staff

First Amendment Anthology
Donald E. Lively, Dorothy E. Roberts, and Russell L. Weaver

International Environmental Law Anthology
Anthony D'Amato and Kirsten Engel

International Human Rights: Law, Policy and Process, Second Edition
Frank C. Newman and David Weissbrodt

**Selected International Human Rights Instruments and
Bibliography For Research on International Human Rights Law, Second Edition**
Frank C. Newman and David Weissbrodt

International Intellectual Property Anthology
Anthony D'Amato and Doris Estelle Long

International Law Anthology
Anthony D'Amato

International Law Coursebook
Anthony D'Amato

Introduction to The Study of Law: Cases and Materials
John Makdisi

Judicial Externships: The Clinic Inside The Courthouse
Rebecca A. Cochran

Justice and the Legal System
A Coursebook
Anthony D'Amato and Arthur J. Jacobson

The Law of Disability Discrimination
Ruth Colker

ADA Handbook
Statutes, Regulations and Related Materials
Publisher's Staff

The Law of Modern Payment Systems and Notes
Fred H. Miller and Alvin C. Harrell

Lawyers and Fundamental Moral Responsibility
Daniel R. Coquillette

Microeconomic Predicates to Law and Economics
Mark Seidenfeld

Patients, Psychiatrists and Lawyers Law and the Mental Health System, Second Edition
Raymond L. Spring, Roy B. Lacoursiere, M.D., and Glen Weissenberger

Principles of Evidence, Third Edition
Irving Younger, Michael Goldsmith, and David A. Sonenshein

Problems and Simulations in Evidence, Second Edition
Thomas F. Guernsey

A Products Liability Anthology
Anita Bernstein

Professional Responsibility Anthology
Thomas B. Metzloff

A Property Anthology
Richard H. Chused

Public Choice and Public Law: Readings and Commentary
Maxwell L. Stearns

Preventive Law: Materials on a Non Adversarial Legal Process
Robert M. Hardaway

The Regulation of Banking
Cases and Materials on Depository Institutions and Their Regulators
Michael P. Malloy

Science in Evidence
David H. Kaye

A Section 1983 Civil Rights Anthology
Sheldon H. Nahmod

Sports Law: Cases and Materials, Third Edition
Ray L. Yasser, James R. McCurdy, and C. Peter Goplerud

A Torts Anthology
Lawrence C. Levine, Julie A. Davies, and Edward J. Kionka

Trial Practice
Lawrence A. Dubin and Thomas F. Guernsey

Trial Practice Problems and Case Files
Edward R. Stein and Lawrence A. Dubin

Trial Practice and Case Files with *Video* Presentation
Edward R. Stein and Lawrence A. Dubin

Unincorporated Business Entities
Larry E. Ribstein

FORTHCOMING PUBLICATIONS

A Civil Procedure Anthology
David I. Levine, Donald L. Doernberg, and Melissa L. Nelken

A Constitutional Law Anthology, Second Edition
Donald E. Lively, Michael J. Glennon, Phoebe A. Haddon, Dorothy E. Roberts,
and Russell L. Weaver

Antitrust Law: Cases and Materials
Daniel J. Gifford and Leo J. Raskind

A Property Law Anthology, Second Edition
Richard H. Chused

Citation Workbook, Second Edition
Maria L. Ciampi, Rivka Widerman, and Vicki Lutz

Constitutional Conflicts, Part II
Derrick A. Bell, Jr.

Contract Law and Practice: Cases and Materials
Michael L. Closen, Gerald E. Berendt, Doris Estelle Long, Marie A. Monahan, Robert J. Nye,
and John H. Scheid

European Union Law Anthology
Anthony D'Amato and Karen V. Kole

Family Law Anthology
Frances E. Olsen

Law and Economics: An Anthology
Kenneth G. Dau-Schmidt and Thomas S. Ulen

PROBLEMS AND SIMULATIONS IN EVIDENCE

. . . .

THOMAS F. GUERNSEY
Associate Dean and Professor of Law
University of Richmond

SECOND EDITION

CINCINNATI
ANDERSON PUBLISHING CO.

GUERNSEY, PROBLEMS AND SIMULATIONS IN EVIDENCE, SECOND EDITION

©1991, 1995 by Anderson Publishing Co.

ISBN: 0-87084-299-4

For Kathe, Alison and Adam

CONTENTS

INTRODUCTION

Using both problems and simulations, this set of materials is designed to teach you to approach evidence in a systematic manner; to analyze both legal doctrine and the factual setting in which that doctrine works. Perhaps the most unique aspect of these materials is the use of simulation. Even in a course like evidence in which faculty have used simulation for many years, most of the simulations used are courtroom simulation. These traditional simulations usually involve direct and cross-examinations. In addition, most traditional simulations are done in the classroom.

While many of the simulations contained in this book are done in the classroom and involve direct and cross-examination, many others involve non-courtroom situations and are designed to be performed outside the classroom. Many of the simulations performed outside the classroom are followed by questionnaires. When these questionnaires are answered after the exercise, they should provide immediate feedback on your understanding of the evidentiary principles involved. Your answers also allow your instructor to judge if the class is having difficulty with the material.

Many of the problems and simulations involve one of the basic fact patterns found in Appendices A - C. Problems beginning *State v. Duffy* refer to Appendix A; *Donato v. Donato* refers to Appendix B; and *Paula v. David and PDG* refers to Appendix C. Where dates involve multiple years, the convention of "Yr - " is used. For example, Yr-0 is the present year and Yr-1 is last year.

I would like to thank several people for help in developing these materials. First, my wife, Kathe Klare, provided me with the special expertise of a nurse-lawyer familiar with both malpractice and laws affecting people with disabilities. Her influence will be seen throughout. Barbara Britzke and I several years ago created the broad outline of the Donato family. The Donato family difficulties, in several different contexts, have engaged students at several law schools for the past fifteen years. Finally, I would like to thank Tony Bocchino and Joe Harbaugh. Tony taught me evidence and how to be a trial lawyer. Joe taught me how to be a teacher.

CHAPTER 1

RELEVANCY

1.1 For each of the following items of proposed evidence, identify the possible factual hypotheses toward which it could be offered and determine whether the evidence should be admissible under Federal Rule of Evidence 401 or under the common law.

[handwritten: yes]

.01 In a prosecution for homicide, the prosecutor seeks to introduce evidence that on two occasions the defendant stated he intended to kill the victim.

[handwritten: yes, hostility]

.02 In an action to quite title, Al claims title by adverse possession. Al seeks to introduce the testimony of two teenagers who will testify that they were told by Al, "Get off this property, it's mine."

[handwritten: yes]

.03 *State v. Duffy.* At Arlo's trial, there is testimony that a chrome plated .38 caliber gun was used in the bank robbery. The prosecutor now seeks to introduce testimony of a neighbor of Arlo's. Although she does not know what type of gun it was, she will testify that she saw the defendant carrying a bright, shiny gun into his apartment two weeks before the robbery. Assume she saw the gun two years before the robbery. Would that affect your answer? Assume Arlo will testify that, at time the neighbor saw him, he had just purchased a set of toy guns for his nephew. Would that change your answer?

[handwritten: yes - damages - not liability]

.04 In a product liability action alleging a defective football helmet, plaintiff claims permanent brain damage resulting in severe emotional problems. These problems, he alleges, include the fact that he is no longer socially active, and that when he does participate in an activity he becomes inordinately tired. Defendant seeks to introduce evidence of plaintiff's post injury sexual and gambling activities.

[handwritten: yes - lawfulness of arrest]

.05 Defendant, a police officer, is sued for violating plaintiff's civil rights during an arrest. Defendant seeks to introduce evidence that plaintiff was using cocaine at the time of the arrest.

[handwritten: Conditional relevance]

.06 Assume that in the preceding question defendant seeks to introduce a picture of a weapon that is allegedly owned by plaintiff. Would it affect your answer if there has not yet been testimony that plaintiff had a gun the night of the arrest?

[handwritten: No - Yes No Scienter]

.07 In a prosecution for knowingly receiving stolen property, the prosecutor seeks to introduce evidence that immediately before defendant made his purchase five other

1

people refused to purchase the property in question. Each of the five people will testify that they believed the property was stolen. Would it make a difference if the five other people were co-workers with the defendant?

No - No Fault

.08 In a workman's compensation case, claimant slipped and fell in a puddle of water. Claimant seeks to introduce testimony that her employer was seen mopping up a puddle in the same location just two hours before she, the claimant, was injured.

No

.09 Defendant is charged with knowingly and willfully making false statements on a passport application. Defendant wishes to introduce evidence that he made the false statements in an attempt to speed up the passport application process so that he could visit his dying mother overseas.

No -

.10 In a defamation action, defendant is alleged to have called the plaintiff, a minister, a "crook." Defendant seeks to introduce evidence that the plaintiff's reputation in the community is that he had frequent affairs with members of his congregation. If the court admits the evidence, what should the plaintiff seek to have the jury instructed?

No - Deep pockets

.11 *Paula v. David and PDG.* Paula seeks to introduce evidence that PDG has liability insurance.

Yes - due to net worth punitive damages

.12 Plaintiff sues a drug manufacturer in an action for personal injury. Under appropriate state law, plaintiff seeks compensation for physical injury, pain, suffering, and punitive damages. Plaintiff seeks to introduce copies of the defendant's financial records, including income tax returns for the preceding five years.

Yes - credibility

.13 *Paula v. David and PDG.* Walter testified that David had the green light. On cross-examination, Brewster asks, "Isn't it true that immediately after the accident you told police officer Kelly that my client, Paula, had the green light?"

.14 During the same cross-examination as in the previous question, Brewster also asks, "Isn't it true that two years ago you had a fight with my client at the Triangle Tavern?"

.15 Following the cross-examination that took place in the two previous questions, Marla asks on redirect examination, "Would you tell the jury why you had the fight with the plaintiff?" [If allowed, the answer will indicate a long standing grudge between the witness and the plaintiff resulting from the plaintiff having fired Walter from a job.]

Yes - routine background authenticating

.16 *Paula v. David and PDG.* Paula calls Wanda to the stand and asks, "How long have you lived here in town?"

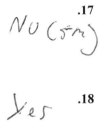

.17 ***State v. Duffy.*** The prosecutor seeks to offer evidence that one hour after the robbery, Arlo fled when he was approached on the street by police officers. Assume the flight occurred five months after the robbery. Would that change your answer?

.18 In the previous question, would it make any difference if it had been reported in the newspapers that Arlo was being sought in connection with a liquor store robbery? Would it make a difference if the newspaper indicated Arlo was sought in connection with a bank robbery?

.19 The state government began condemnation proceedings against a landowner's property, and introduced testimony by an expert appraiser that the landowner's property is worth $100,000. The landowner seeks to introduce testimony from a local real estate agent that in the past three years five houses have been sold in same neighborhood, each for a price in excess of $110,000.

1.2 For each of the following pieces of evidence, identify the possible factual hypotheses toward which it could be offered and whether the evidence should be admissible under Federal Rules of Evidence 401 and 403, or the common law.

.01 Plaintiff sued defendant for running him over with his car as he attempted to cross an intersection. Plaintiff seeks to introduce a color photograph of himself which shows him on the street with blood flowing from his head.

.02 Plaintiff, a nationally known religious/political figure, sues the owner of a men's magazine for defamation and invasion of privacy. The allegedly defamatory comments were made in the magazine in the context of an advertising parody. Plaintiff seeks to introduce the entire magazine, containing numerous "hard core" pictures of people in various stages of undress and sexual activity.

.03 In defendant's trial for illegal possession of marijuana, the prosecutor seeks to introduce expert evidence concerning the effects of the drug.

.04 A border patrol officer is charged with obtaining sexual favors from illegal aliens in return for allowing them to enter the country. The defendant seeks to introduce evidence that the illegal aliens were formerly employed as prostitutes.

.05 Plaintiff's son died, allegedly from inhaling a household product made by the defendant. Defendant seeks to introduce evidence of the son's marijuana use.

.06 Plaintiff sued the manufacturer of an automobile for personal injuries, alleging a design defect. Plaintiff seeks to introduce the longitudinal cross section of a new car of the same model in an attempt to show the jury the manufacturing defect.

.07   Defendant is charged with the murder of his wife and two children. Defendant claims that drug crazed people broke into his house the night of the murders, and that, after he was unsuccessful in fighting them off, they killed his family. The prosecutor requests the judge allow the jury view the defendant's home where the murders occurred.

.08   ***Paula v. David and PDG.*** Paula's attorney asks the judge to allow the jury to go to the intersection and view the accident scene.

.09   In a product liability action, plaintiff claims his leg was severed when defendant's machine malfunctioned. Plaintiff seeks to exhibit his leg to the jury.

.10   In an action against defendant for child abuse, the prosecutor seeks to introduce color photographs of the child showing bruises and cigarette burns.

.11   Defendant is charged with receiving illegal "kickbacks" from vendors. Defendant wishes to call 78 vendors who will each testify that defendant did not solicit kickbacks from them, and that they did not pay any kickbacks to the defendant.

1.3   Defendants are on trial for conspiracy to damage, and destroy by fire, a building used in interstate commerce and of actually damaging and destroying the building. The prosecution seeks, over defendants' objection, to show that the building in question had four other fires over a three year period.

.01   Under what circumstances, if any, should evidence of these four fires be admitted? What is the judge's role in making this determination of admissibility?

.02   If the trial court admits the evidence, what should defense counsel do to preserve her objection for appeal?

.03   Assume the court conducted a *voir dire* hearing on the issue. If a defendant testifies during this hearing denying any connection with the four previous fires, has the defendant waived his right to refuse to testify concerning whether he committed the crime for which he is now being tried?

.04   Should this *voir dire* examination take place in the presence of the jury?

1.4   Douglass, a black woman, was an hourly employee at defendant's manufacturing plant. She had 12 years seniority. Douglass was involved in a fight at work with two white co-workers, Robert and Jan McCrossen. As a result of the fight, Douglass was fired. Neither of the McCrossens were discharged. Prior to the present action, she had received no reprimands or any form of discipline.

After exhausting administrative remedies, Douglass brought the present action, alleging that her discharge was discriminatory.

At trial, Douglass, over objection of the defendant, introduced evidence of fights involving other employees of the defendant, including what disciplinary action, if any, was taken by the defendant. She alleges that the evidence demonstrates a pattern of disparate treatment against racial minorities by the defendant. This evidence includes:

> 1. A fight between a black male and a white male that took place ten years earlier. There was conflicting evidence as to who started the fight. Company records show that after the two men exchanged heated words, the black man struck the white man, and the white man swung a wild blow at the other, but missed hitting him. The Company then discharged both men, but later reinstated the white man, reducing his penalty to a 30 day suspension.

> 2. Only one employee has been discharged by the Company for engaging in a physical altercation at the workplace. This happened ten years ago when the man had gone home early, but returned to the plant intoxicated and attacked a plant foreman.

> 3. Two white employees were involved in a fight nine years ago. One was hospitalized. Both were suspended.

> 4. Eight years ago a white employee struck a co-worker who was also white, "after provocation," according to company records. The employee was suspended for one week.

> 5. Seven years ago a Mexican-American hit a white employee in the face. The Company discharged the Mexican-American employee, though both employees told the company that they were merely goofing around.

> 6. Two black employees were engaged in a fight six years ago. One was given a four day suspension.

> 7. A white male had a fight with his supervisor two years ago and was subsequently given a one day disciplinary layoff.

The jury returned a verdict for plaintiff. In granting defendant's motion for a judgment notwithstanding the verdict, the trial court stated:

> The evidence of past incidents was irrelevant. Of the thirteen employees discussed by the plaintiff in her case-in-chief, only two are truly similarly situated to the plaintiff all three, including plaintiff, were unprovoked aggressors. None of the other eleven employee examples were involved in similar circumstances, mainly because none of the eleven but Robinson was adjudged by the defendant an aggressor. Based on these conclusions, I hold that plaintiff presented absolutely no evidence which met the test of relevance.

Is plaintiff's evidence relevant? Is it appropriate to rule the evidence admissible during plaintiff's case-in-chief and then to reverse that decision in ruling on the motion for the judgment notwithstanding the verdict? Reread the trial court's rationale, does it suggest some confusion as to the appropriate role of the judge *vis-a-vis* the jury?

1.5   **Fact Investigation.** *State v. Duffy.* You have just been assigned to prosecute Arlo Duffy. You must now begin your fact investigation of the case. You will need to tell the investigators what they should look for. Identify the key legal or factual propositions or hypotheses crucial to both prosecuting and defending the bank robbery charge. Itemize the specific evidence from witnesses, as well as the demonstrative and physical evidence you expect the investigator to gather, relating to each of these factual propositions. Be sure to indicate where and how the investigator should look for this evidence.

1.6   **Fact Investigation.** *Donato v. Donato.* You represent Gina. You must now begin your fact investigation of the case. You will need to instruct the investigators on what they should look for. Identify the key legal or factual propositions crucial to both the mother and father in the custody case. Itemize the specific evidence from witnesses, as well as the demonstrative and physical evidence you expect the investigator to gather, relating to these factual propositions. Be sure to indicate where and how he should look for this evidence.

1.7   **Closing Argument.** *State v. Duffy.* You represent Arlo. Based on the material contained in the *State v. Duffy* file, make your *closing* argument to the jury.

1.8   **Legislative Drafting.** You work for a state legislator on a committee considering the adoption of rules of evidence modeled after the Federal Rules. The legislator has asked you to consider the appropriateness of redrafting Federal Rule 401's "any tendency" language with language setting a higher standard of probativeness. Prepare to discuss this with the legislator, being sure to consider whether such a revision is appropriate, and, if the legislator determines it is, what the standard ought to be and how the rule should be rewritten.

CHAPTER 2

COMPETENCY, PERSONAL KNOWLEDGE
AND OATH OR AFFIRMATION

2.1   Basic Competency Concepts.

.01   Six year old Alice was allegedly raped by her father. The father is on trial. Should Alice be allowed to testify? What factors should go into the decision as to whether she may testify?

.02   ***State v. Duffy.*** Before his arrest, the police received a tip from Beatrice Duke that Arlo had told her he had committed the robbery. Beatrice takes the stand, and defense counsel objects to her testimony on the ground that she is incompetent to testify because she is addicted to heroin. Assuming she is addicted, how should the judge rule?

.03   ***State v. Duffy.*** Arlo takes the stand and denies all involvement in the robbery. During the cross-examination of Arlo, the judge interjects the following:

Q: Excuse me, Mr. Duffy. Didn't you call me about a week before your arrest?

A: Yes, your honor.

Q: You came by my office too?

A: Yes, sir.

Q: You wanted help?

A: I haven't ever been in trouble like this.

Q: I told you to simply tell the truth, didn't I?

A: Yes.

Q: You said you couldn't because other people were involved?

A: I think, as best I can remember, that I told you the same as I testified today.

Q: But you told me a different story then didn't you?

Was this questioning proper? If not, what should defense counsel do?

.04   In a criminal prosecution, the defendant moved for a mistrial claiming the defendant was denied the presumption of innocence. To support the motion, defense counsel seeks to call as a witness a juror sitting in the case. The juror, if allowed, will testify that she saw the defendant in the parking lot of the courthouse during a lunch break. At the time, the defendant was wearing handcuffs. May the juror testify?

.05   Following a verdict of guilty in a federal criminal prosecution, a member of the jury contacted defense counsel. The juror told counsel that she was sorry the defendant was convicted. The foreman of the jury, however, scared her to death with his demands that a decision be made and his unwillingness to accept any discussion that the defendant was not guilty. In an attempt to set aside the verdict, defense counsel seeks to call this former juror as a witness. Should the judge allow the testimony? Assume the juror told defense counsel that the foreman had brought in copies of the newspaper during deliberations and used press accounts to support his argument that the defendant was guilty. Could the juror now be called in support of defendant's motion?

.06   ***Donato v. Donato.*** Gina's lawyer interviewed the children prior to trial. Richard indicated that, although he did not approve of his mother's relationship with Sam Gordon, Sam was always interested in Richard's activities and seemed to care about Allen and Ellen. At trial, however, Richard testifies that Sam always complains to Gina about the other kids, and that it seemed that he (Richard) could never do anything right when he and Sam were together. On cross-examination, by Mrs. Donato's lawyer, the following occurs:

Q: Richard, you have been staying with your father for the week before this hearing, is that right?

A: Yes.

Q: In fact, he just bought you a car, didn't he?

A: That's right.

Q: Now Richard, you remember talking to me in my office two weeks ago?

A: Yes.

Q: We were alone, isn't that right?

A: Yes.

Q: At that time Richard, didn't you tell me that Sam had always been interested in Richard's activities and seemed to care for Allen and Ellen?

A: No. I would never have said that.

When Mrs. Donato next has the opportunity to call witnesses, may her lawyer testify that Richard had indeed made the above statement to her in her office?

2.2   Witness Interview. *State v. Duffy.* You represent the defendant, Arlo Duffy. According to the police report, Roy Smith was a witness to the bank robbery. The police did not have Roy try to identify Arlo in the lineup for reasons that follow. Roy, however, has been listed as a witness who will be testifying for the prosecution.

The police did not have Roy attempt an identification of Arlo, because Roy was not suppose to be in front of the bank when he was there. Roy is a resident of the state mental institution located in the city where the robbery occurred. Roy was involuntarily committed to the institution two years ago with a diagnosis of paranoid schizophrenia. This is the latest in a series of hospitalizations which began fifteen years ago. The recent commitment, instituted by his children, was precipitated by Roy's fear of being victimized by criminals. Roy had locked himself in his one bedroom apartment, literally nailing the door closed and boarding the windows. It took his children three days to convince Roy to let them enter the apartment. When they did enter, they found Roy curled in a corner of the room holding a gun and crying.

You have made an appointment to interview Roy in anticipation of trial. Your task is to gather as much information as you can concerning Roy's proposed testimony, and to evaluate Roy's competency to testify at trial. **Your instructor will provide the person playing Roy with confidential information. Be sure to fill out the joint questionnaire following the simulation.**

2.3   Witness Interview. *Donato v. Donato.* You are a law student clerking for the attorney that represents Mrs. Donato. Your supervising partner is considering having Allen Donato testify at the custody hearing concerning the events that occurred in Paul's apartment during the storm. One concern of your partner is whether Allen would be considered competent to testify. You have, therefore, been instructed to interview Allen. Your task is to gather as much information as you can concerning Allen's competency to testify. You have made an appointment to meet with Allen. Mrs. Donato has agreed to let you speak to him alone. **Your instructor will provide the person playing**

Allen with confidential information. Be sure to fill out the joint questionnaire following the simulation.

2.4   Defendant is on trial for abduction and murder. The defendant files a pretrial motion to exclude the testimony of Tyrone Griffin, because hypnosis was used to refresh or attempt to refresh his memory. Griffin was apparently the last person to see the victim alive. He can testify, among other things, that he saw her get into a sports car approximately three hours before her body was found. At the hearing on the motion, it was established that a physician attempted to hypnotize Griffin. The physician then prompted Griffin to give a more detailed account of the day's events by intervening with questions as Griffin narrated the day's events. Police officers present during the hypnosis session testified that the physician's questions were not suggestive. The police also testified that the only new piece of information obtained during the session was the color of the car that Griffin saw the victim drive away in on the day of the alleged abduction. What result on defendant's motion? Suppose instead of attempting to hypnotize the witness before trial, the prosecutor seeks to hypnotize the witness while on the witness stand. If defense counsel objects, what ruling?

2.5   *Paula v. David and PDG.* Assume that on cross-examination of Walter the following takes place:

> Q: Just before the accident, you were in the Triangle Tavern, weren't you?

> A: Yes.

> Q: You were there for an hour?

> A: About that.

> Q: You had four double vodkas, isn't that right?

> A: I wasn't counting.

> Q: You wouldn't deny that you had that many, would you?

> A: No, that sounds about right.

> Q: Your honor, at this point I move to strike the witness's testimony on direct examination on the basis that he did not have firsthand knowledge.

How should the judge rule?

2.6   On the issue of the location of a meeting, John Dean testifies that, "It was at the Mayflower Hotel, I think. I'm not positive, though. It could have been at the Shoreham which has a Mayflower restaurant." Opposing counsel objects. What ruling?

2.7   Action in Tax Court, which under the Internal Revenue Code follows Federal Rule of Evidence 603. The standard oath used in the court states:

> I [witness name] do solemnly swear or affirm that the testimony I am about to give
> will be the truth, the whole truth, and nothing but the truth, so help me God.

The taxpayer calls a witness who, for religious reasons refuses to use the word "solemnly" in her oath. The Government objects to her testifying. What result? A second witness called by the taxpayer states "I can't take the oath if it has God's name in it. If you ask me if I'll tell the truth, I can say that." The Government objects to her testifying. What result? A third witness refuses to use the words "swear or affirm." The Government objects to her testifying. What result? A fourth witness refuses to take any oath at all. The judge asks her whether she will say, "I state that I will tell the truth in my testimony"? She refuses. The Government objects to her testifying. What result?

2.8   In a criminal prosecution, the prosecutor seeks to introduce a tape of a telephone conversation. The conversation is completely in Spanish. The prosecutor, therefore, seeks to introduce a transcript of the tape that has been translated into English. The translator is called to the witness stand. What type of oath should be administered?

2.9   Defendant is on trial for conspiracy to distribute cocaine. The prosecution calls a witness William Earl McDonald. McDonald is sworn taking a standard oath that ends "so help me God." On cross-examination, McDonald admits he is an atheist. Defendant moves to strike McDonald's testimony. On questioning by the judge, McDonald then testifies that he took the oath seriously, that he respected the oath, and that "to the best of my ability, I'm telling the truth." What ruling on defendant's motion to strike?

CHAPTER 3

FORM OF THE QUESTION

3.1 **Direct Examination.** *State v. Duffy.* Arlo Duffy is on trial and the prosecutor has called Glenda Berg to the stand as the first witness. The following is a transcript of her testimony. Answer the questions associated with each objection.

[The witness was sworn]

Q: Would you tell us your name?

A: Glenda Berg.

Q: And where do you live?

A: 121 Elm St., here in Calhoun.

Q: How long have you lived there?

A: Five years.

Q: You work at First Investors on Main St. as a senior teller, is that right?

Defense Attorney: Objection, your honor, leading.

.01   State the correct ruling and the reason(s) for the ruling.

Q: How long have you worked there?

A: Four years, no actually three or three and a half.

Q: Directing your attention to June 1, Yr-0, at approximately 1:30 p.m., were you working?

Defense Attorney: Objection, your honor, leading

.02   State the correct ruling and the reason(s) for the ruling.

Q: Starting at the beginning and taking us step by step through the events, could you tell the jury what happened at approximately 1:30?

Sustained – narrative

Defense Attorney: Objection, your honor.

.03   State the possible ground(s) for objection, the correct ruling, and the reason for the ruling.

A: I was working in the bank when a man came into the building.

Q: When did you first notice the defendant?   *fact not in evidence*

Defense Attorney: Objection, your honor.

.04   State the ground(s) for objection, the correct ruling, and the reason for the ruling.

A: I first noticed him as he walked in the door.

Q: About how far away from him were you?

A: No more than thirty-five feet.

Q: Why did you happen to notice him?

A: Well there were no other customers in the bank at the time and he had this hat in his hands. Well, actually is was ski cap, you know, one of those wool or knit things that pull over your head with holes for the eyes and nose.

Q: Beginning from the point where you first noticed the man, tell us everything that happened?   *narrative*

Defense Attorney: Objection, your honor.

.05   State the ground(s) for objection, the correct ruling, and the reason for the ruling.

A: Well, I thought something was going to happen because he was carrying this hat and before I knew it he had pulled it over his head.

Q: After he pulled the ski cap over his head, what happened?

A: I immediately pressed the silent alarm and called Ms. Dodge.

Q: Did the man go to your or Ms. Van Donk's window first?

Defense Attorney: Objection, your honor.   *Assumes fact not in evidence (Leading)*

.06   State the ground(s) for objection, the correct ruling, and the reason for the ruling.

A: The man went to Sherry Van Donk's window first, and then came to mine.

Q: Who is Ms. Van Donk?

A: She is the other teller who was working in the bank on the day of the robbery?

Q: Were you able to <u>see and hear</u> what he said to Ms. Van Donk?

Compoved quest

Defense Attorney: Objection, your honor.

.07   State the ground(s) for objection, the correct ruling, and the reason for the ruling.

A: No, I just saw Sherry put money into his leather briefcase.

Q: What happened then?

overruled

Defense Attorney: Objection, your honor, assuming a fact not in evidence.

.08   State the correct ruling, and the reason for the ruling.

A: He came over to my window.

Q: And?

A: He pointed a big gun in my face.

Q: Did he say anything?

A: He didn't say anything, just pointed that big gun at me, and I gave him what money I had.

Q: What happened then?

A: He turned and ran away.

Q: Where did he run?

A: Out the door, back to Main Street.

Q: Now, Ms. Berg, you mentioned he had a gun. Was its barrel shiny like chrome, dark blue, or some other color?

Defense Attorney: Objection, your honor.

.09   State the ground(s) for objection, the correct ruling, and the reason for the ruling.

Q: Could you describe its barrel? Was it long or short?   *Leading*

Defense Attorney: Objection, your honor.

.10   State the ground(s) for objection, the correct ruling, and the reason for the ruling.

A: Long, maybe 6 inches.

Q: You also mentioned the briefcase. Could you describe it?

A: Yes. It was leather, a burgundy color. It looked like a hand sewn thing, you know, the kind you'd buy at a craft shop — real leather. It was maybe two inches thick and a rectangle, maybe 18 inches long and 12 inches wide. I think it closed with a buckle.

Q: Did it have a handle or did you carry it some other way?

Defense Attorney: Objection, your honor.   *Leading*

.11   State the ground(s) for objection, the correct ruling, and the reason for the ruling.

A: It had a handle, a strap about one inch wide and maybe eight inches long.

Q: Are you able to describe the robber?

A: He was a white guy, I'd say in his late twenties, but that's just a guess. You know his shape made him look on the young side. He was maybe 5'9" or so, and 160 lbs.

Q: Excuse me, was that 5'9"?

Defense Attorney: Objection, your honor.   *Argumentative*

.12   State the ground(s) for objection, the correct ruling, and the reason for the ruling.

Q: You testified earlier that he came right up to your window; so you had a pretty good view of him?

Defense Attorney: Objection, your honor.   *Leading*
Argumentative

.13   State the ground(s) for objection, the correct ruling, and the reason for the ruling.

> Q: I have no further questions, thank you.

3.2   *Paula v. David and PDG.* May Paula call David as a witness and ask, "Isn't it true that on January 15, of last year, at approximately 4:15 p.m., you were driving a truck owned by the defendant?", and "You were on company business at the time weren't you?" *yes _ oK*

3.3   Defendant is on trial for shoplifting a watch. On direct examination, the prosecutor calls as a witness the companion of the defendant on the day of the alleged shoplifting. The Prosecutor asks the question, "Isn't it true that you saw the defendant place the gold watch in his pocket?" Defendant objects. What ruling and why? Assume the witness had previously refused to speak to the prosecutor. Would that affect your answer? *leading* *Chostule ok*
                    √ surprise ?

3.4   Assume that the questions in 3.2 were allowed, and that the plaintiff's lawyer did not ask any additional questions. On cross-examination, David's lawyer asks the following questions. Should they be permitted over a timely objection?

> Q: Isn't it true that you normally get off work at 3:30?
>
> Q: You've lived and worked in this city for 10 years, haven't you?
>
> Q: Plaintiff hit you, didn't she?
>
> Q: You didn't see plaintiff before she struck you, did you?
>
> Q: Was plaintiff in the intersection when you struck her?

may own Evan
of Pl,d client
Rule authod
611

3.5   Law Professor Arrested for Robbery. Your client is your evidence professor. He or she is charged with driving the get-away car in an armed robbery of a bank at the corner of Main and Third Streets at 3:00 p.m. August 26, Yr - 0. As the professor's lawyer, you should attempt to elicit all the information contained in this statement. All students not doing the direct examination should object to all improperly formed questions, being prepared to state the reason for the objection.

* * *

My name is _____ and I live at _____. I am employed as a Professor at _____ Law School. On August 26, Yr-0, I was so employed and arrived at the law school at approximately 7:30 a.m. The reason I was late was that I had received a long distance phone call at home from an old professor of mine who needed help preparing for his class. I went immediately to my office to prepare for evidence.

At 9:00 a.m., I received a call from the director of the local legal services office concerning a proposed training conference. We arranged a meeting for 1:45 at my office. At 10:00 I went to the other class I teach besides evidence and taught until 10:50. Students had lots of questions after class so I did not get back to my office until 12:00 noon. I stayed in my office until 2:00 p.m., when the director of legal services showed up (fifteen minutes late). We talked for fifteen minutes and then went to lunch at the Peking Restaurant at the corner of Main and Third Streets. I drove my car, a blue Toyota. The Peking is located just diagonally across from the bank that was apparently robbed. At about 3:15, we finished lunch and as we left the restaurant, I heard sirens and saw a blue subcompact car go speeding by me on Third Street. Its license number was XYZ 999.

At 3:30 p.m., I returned to my office to prepare for the next day's evidence class. At 4:30 I had coffee with Professor _____ in her office. At 5:00 I returned to my office to work on my evidence treatise. I stayed in my office until 8:00 p.m. I had to leave early that night to go to a social gathering of faculty in the faculty lounge celebrating the beginning of a new academic year. I stayed there until about 10:00 p.m., then went home.

At 11:00 p.m., while I was reviewing the galleys of my most recent article, the police knocked on my door and arrested me for robbing a bank on Main at Third. I don't know anything about any robbery. That is the truth.

/s/ *Professor* _____

3.6   *State v. Duffy.* Prepare the direct examination of Sherry Van Donk. Be sure to establish her credibility, set the scene to which she will testify and elicit a narrative of her testimony. It is also usually wise to elicit any unfavorable testimony rather than waiting until the cross-examiner brings it out.

3.7   Refer to problem 3.5. Assume the Professor can not remember the color of the subcompact car. Refresh his or her recollection using the statement to the police. How else might you refresh his or her recollection?

CHAPTER 4

HEARSAY

A. The Hearsay Rule

4.1 The Basic Concept. For each of the following indicate whether the evidence is hearsay.

   .01   *Paula v. David and PDG.* On the issue of whether the light was green for David, the witness will testify that Walter told him the light was green for David.

   .02   *State v. Duffy.* On the issue of what the bank robber looked like, the prosecutor seeks to introduce the signed statement of Sherry Van Donk.

   .03   *State v. Duffy.* On the issue of how many people were in the bank at the time of the robbery, Officer Gorham will testify that Sherry Van Donk told him that there were five customers in the bank.

   .04   In an action to quiet title, the plaintiff seeks to introduce testimony that he told a group of teenagers, "I own this property, now get off."

   .05   In an action for defamation, brought by a priest, the defendant is alleged to have said that the priest frequents a house of prostitution. Defendant wishes to introduce evidence that the priest's reputation in the community is that he is unchaste.

   .06   *State v. Duffy.* On the issue of how many people were in the bank at the time of the robbery, Sherry Van Donk will testify that she told Officer Gorham that there were five customers in the bank.

   .07   On the issue of whether Charlie was one of a group of boys who were at a party on Tuesday night, the high school principal will testify, "I went to Charlie's classroom on Wednesday morning and asked the entire class, who was at the party Tuesday night? Charlie raised his hand."

   .08   On the issue of whether Charlie did not like Charlotte, Harold will testify that Charlie told him that he hated Charlotte.

   .09   On the issue of whether Charlie did not like Charlotte, Harold will testify that Charlie told him that he, Charlie, thought Charlotte was a liar.

.10   ***State v. Duffy.*** On the issue of whether there were gun shots associated with the robbery, defense counsel seeks to have a private investigator testify that he talked to people in the bank, and in businesses close by, and that no one heard any gunshots.

.11   Plaintiff brought suit challenging the constitutionality of a federal statute that prohibits political committees from spending more than a set sum on behalf of political candidates. To establish the government's interest in passing the statute, the government seeks to introduce a magazine article that reported several people interviewed in Washington, D.C., said that numerous top officials in the executive branch got their jobs by making significant contributions to political campaigns.

.12   On the issue of whether the parties entered into a contract, the plaintiff seeks to introduce testimony that he told the defendant, "That sounds great, I'll take all the widgets you've got at your price of $25 each."

.13   Former friends dispute the ownership of an antique gun. Ben claims the gun was a gift from Al. Al claims he merely let Ben borrow the gun and now wants it back. The gun, Al claims, was a family heirloom given to him by his father. Ben will testify Al came to his house and, handing the gun to Ben said, "You've been a good friend. Here I want you to have this."

.14   In a criminal prosecution for income tax evasion, defendant wishes to testify that she was told by her accountant that it was proper to take certain deductions.

.15   Defendant, a convicted felon, is charged with illegal possession of a firearm. Defendant was arrested during a lawful search of his father's house. Defendant was holding the gun at the time of his arrest. One element of the crime is that defendant was not justified in possessing the firearm. Defendant claims that the gun is his father's. He claims he only picked it up because he thought the police were really a neighborhood gang breaking into his father's house. To rebut this claim, the prosecutor wishes to introduce testimony of a police officer who will say, "I was at the back door of the house, in order to keep anyone from fleeing. Officer Smith was in the front of the house. At 8:30 a.m. sharp, I heard Officer Smith yell, 'This is the police. Open up!'"

.16   In the previous problem, assume defendant did not have the gun in his hand. During the search of the house, the police found a holster and gun in a dresser which defendant admits is where he keeps his clothes. The holster has initials inscribed on it that are the same as the defendant's. On the issue of whether the defendant possessed the gun, the prosecutor seeks to introduce the holster and gun.

.17   ***Paula v. David and P.D.G..*** To prove what time the accident occurred, Walter seeks to testify that the clock on the nearby bank indicated that it was 1:00 p.m.

.18   *Paula v. David and PDG.* To prove what time the accident occurred, Walter seeks to testify that the clock in the nearby church tower chimed once, indicating that it was 1:00 p.m.

.19   *Paula v. David and PDG.* To prove what time the accident occurred, Walter seeks to testify that he thought the time might be important, so as a soon as he saw the accident, he stopped his watch. Later that day he looked at it and it was stopped at 1:00 p.m.

.20   To prove that one bid on a government contract was received before another, a party seeks to introduce the two bids, each of which was stamped by a secretary using a time and date machine.

4.2   **A Bit More Complicated.** For each of the following, indicate whether the evidence is hearsay.

.01   In a criminal prosecution for homicide, the defendant, Harry, asserts a claim of self defense and seeks to introduce testimony that the victim had a reputation in the community as a violent person. Further, Harry seeks to have a witness testify that he, the witness, heard the victim tell a group of people, "Harry's a dead man. I'm out to get him."

.02   *State v. Duffy.* On the issue of whether Arlo Duffy believes he is guilty, Roy Smith will testify that at the time the robbery was taking place, he saw Arlo running away from the bank.

.03   In a murder prosecution, a police officer proposes to testify that the day after the murder he went to the defendant's house and asked the defendant's mother to give him the clothes defendant wore the previous day. The mother gave the officer a set of clothing. The prosecutor seeks to have the clothes introduced.

.04   Plaintiff, a physician, sues defendant insurance company on the theory of bad faith failure to settle within the policy limits of the plaintiff's medical malpractice insurance coverage. Plaintiff seeks to introduce a letter from her to the insurance company in which she stated, "I am in receipt of your letter indicating that my former patient Mr. Smith is willing to settle this matter for $500,000. This is well within my policy limits and I hereby give you notice that you should accept his offer to settle."

4.3   What's The Proposition? For each of the following indicate whether the evidence is hearsay.

.01   ***Paula v. David and PDG.*** Walter testifies on direct examination that David had the green light. On cross-examination, Brewster asks, "Isn't it true that immediately after the accident you told the police officer the light was red for the defendant?"

.02   ***State v. Duffy.*** Officer Gorham will testify that when he approached Arlo, then a suspect in the criminal investigation, and asked his name, Arlo responded, "Al Smith."

.03   Defendant is charged with mail fraud and asserts as a defense lack of intent. The prosecutor seeks to introduce evidence of complaints of mail fraud to the Better Business Bureau made by customers of the defendant over the course of several years.

.04   Plaintiff brings an action against an airline and an airplane manufacturer arising out of an airplane crash. The accident was allegedly caused by an explosion resulting from a leaking fuel line. Plaintiff seeks to introduce the flight checklist of the pilot in which the pilot indicated that the fuel line had a leak. Plaintiff also seeks to introduce the testimony of a janitor working at the airport who will testify that he heard a mechanic tell the pilot, "the fuel line has a leak," and the pilot responded, "That's okay, it's something in the way they designed the stupid thing. It always leaks a bit."

.05   In a prosecution for perjury, the prosecutor seeks to introduce the grand jury transcript containing the statement alleged to constitute perjury.

.06   In problem 4.1.05, plaintiff seeks to introduce the testimony of Walker who, if allowed, will testify that he heard the defendant say that the plaintiff was unchaste.

.07   In the previous problem, plaintiff seeks to introduce the testimony of Walker who, if allowed, will testify that he heard Debra say that the defendant said that the plaintiff was unchaste.

.08   Assume that in the previous problem, plaintiff is suing both the original defendant and Debra.

4.4 Some Problem Areas. For each of the following indicate whether the evidence is hearsay.

.01   A man, Max Klinger, in order to get a psychiatric discharge from the army, needs to prove that he is insane. Max wants to introduce testimony from a witness who will testify that Max always goes around saying "I'm a woman, and I shouldn't be in the Army." Max also wants to introduce testimony from a witness who will testify that Max always wears dresses. Finally, Max wishes to introduce testimony from a witness who will state, "Max comes to talk to me. He is very concerned about whether he should adopt, since he was having trouble getting pregnant."

.02   ***State v. Duffy.*** The prosecutor offers a police investigator who will testify that when questioned, Arlo's mother indicated that Arlo was with her on the day of the robbery. The investigator, however, will also say he has a videotape of Arlo at party at his apartment on the day of the robbery.

B. Prior Statements

Propety   *Yes – Sworn Statement*

4.5   Defendant is charged with violation of the immigration laws by aiding several foreign nationals in attempts to enter the country illegally. The aliens, driving a van registered in defendant's name, were apprehended by the Border Patrol and taken to the Patrol's station house. The aliens then made tape recorded, sworn statements implicating the defendant in their illegal entry. At trial, the aliens denied that defendant was involved in the illegal entry. Are the statements made to the Border Patrol admissible under FRE 801(d)(1)(A)? Can these statements be distinguished from statements made by witnesses to police officers at a station house? Is there any additional information you would like to know?

4.6   ***Paula v. David and PDG.*** On direct examination, Wanda testifies that David was speeding just before the accident. On cross-examination, Wanda is asked: *witness*

> Q: Didn't you tell the police on the day of the accident that David was driving at the speed limit?
>
> A: Yes.
>
> Q: Isn't it true that you began dating the plaintiff two weeks ago?
>
> A: Yes.

On redirect, the witness is asked:

> Q: Have you ever told anyone else how fast David was driving at the time of the accident?
>
> A: Yes.

Q: When was this?

A: About four weeks ago.

Q: Who did you tell this to?

A: You, when came to my house and asked me some questions.

Q: What did you tell me?

The defense counsel then objected. Paula's counsel makes an offer of proof that, if allowed to testify, the witness will state, "As I explained to you then, I had gotten mixed up at the accident scene about whose car was whose, and made a mistake. I told you David was speeding." How should the judge rule? Assume the conversation with the lawyer occurred just one week ago. What ruling?

4.7   Defendant, already convicted and serving time in prison on another charge, was indicted for possession of marijuana. An element the prosecutor needs to establish is that the defendant was aware of the marijuana that was found in his locker in the prison dormitory. A corrections officer, Castello, testified that after the marijuana was found, he took the defendant to a different cell and on the way there the defendant stated, "Alright, you got me now. Tell me who fingered me." On cross-examination of Castello, the following occurred:

Q: Officer Castello, you wrote a report of this incident didn't you?

A: Yes.

Q: That's the same report you referred to on direct examination?

A: Yes

Q: Could you point out where in that report it says the defendant made the statement, "Tell me who fingered me"?

A: That statement is not in the report.

The government then calls a second corrections officer who testifies that on the day the drugs were seized he had been told by officer Castello that the defendant said, "Tell me who fingered me." Defense counsel objects. What is the proper ruling?

4.8   Doug is charged with the rape of Alice. Alice is the nine year old daughter of Doug's girlfriend. On direct examination, Alice testifies that Doug raped her. On cross-examination of Alice, defense counsel asks:

Q: You visit your Daddy a lot, don't you Alice?

A: Yes.

Q: You like going to visit him?

A: Yes.

Q: Now, I know this may be hard for you to say in front of everybody, but it's important. You would prefer to live with your Daddy wouldn't you?

A: I love my mommy.

In rebuttal, the prosecutor seeks to call Mary who, if allowed, will testify that after the defendant was indicted, but before trial, Alice told her (Mary) that Doug raped her (Alice).

4.9   *State v. Duffy.*

.01   Sherry Van Donk takes the witness stand and testifies, "I went down to the police station and saw a bunch of guys in, I guess, what they call a lineup and I told them that it was that guy Duffy that robbed the bank." Is this admissible?

.02   Assume instead of the teller, a police offer takes that stand and says, "Ms. Van Donk came to the station to view a line up and she said that Arlo Duffy was the one who robbed the bank." Is this admissible?

.03   Assume that Ms. Van Donk denies ever having identified Arlo Duffy as the robber. May the police officer testify as in the previous question?

.04   The prosecutor calls a police officer to the stand to introduce a letter purportedly signed by Harold Johnson which states that the writer was standing at his window when he saw Arlo run out of the bank carrying a brief case. Is this admissible?

.05   Arlo has brown eyes. On cross-examination, Sherry Van Donk testifies that she does not remember the color of the robber's eyes. On cross-examination, Officer Mundy is asked by defense counsel, "Isn't it true that Ms. Van Donk told you that the robber's eyes were blue?" The prosecutor objects, what ruling?

C. Admissions

4.10   For each of the following, indicate whether the evidence is hearsay at common law or an admission under the Federal Rules of Evidence. If it is hearsay at common law, is it admissible as an admission of a party opponent?

.01   Plaintiff, in a suit involving an intersection collision, is alleged to have negligently entrusted his automobile to his daughter and therefore was contributorily negligent. Defendant wishes to introduce the testimony of Denise who will state that she overheard plaintiff tell his neighbor, "I don't know what to do with my daughter. She is just so reckless in the car."

next

.02   Refer to problem 4.1.13. Al seeks to call Walter who will testify that he, Walter, went hunting with Ben and Ben told him that "Al's great, he's letting me use this antique gun."

.03   Reconsider 4.2.02.

.04   Defendants Nash and Coco are on trial for violation of anti-loan sharking laws and the murder of Victor. The prosecutor calls Walter to the stand to testify that he, Walter, asked Nash and Coco whatever happened to Victor? Walter will testify that Nash said, "He fell in to the canal -- no one cared," and that Coco "just smiled."

.05   *Paula v. David and PDG.* Paula initially alleged in her complaint that the weather was cold and raining. Later, pursuant to a provision similar to Federal Rule of Civil Procedure 15, Paula amended her complaint to allege that the weather was clear and dry. As required under local procedural rules, Paula signed the complaint. Defendants seek to introduce into evidence the superseded complaint.

admis party

.06   *Paula v. David and PDG.* Assume Paula first sued David and PDG alleging in the complaint that the weather was cold and raining. As required under local procedural rules, Paula signed the complaint. Paula subsequently sued Walter, alleging Walter caused the accident by darting out into the street. Walter seeks to introduce the complaint filed in the suit against David and PDG.

Yes

.07   Plaintiff sued defendant in a civil action for assault and battery. Plaintiff wishes to introduce the guilty plea defendant entered in a criminal assault and battery action arising out of the same actions causing plaintiff to bring her suit.

4.11   *Paula v. David and PDG.* Paula claims a back injury resulting from the accident. Defendants contend the back injury was a preexisting condition, and seek to introduce a health form attached to Paula's application for college. The form, signed by a physician two years ago, indicates an abnormal back. Paula objects to the introduction of the form. What ruling? Assume that instead of being attached to an application for college, the form was filled out by a physician as part of Paula's application for a summer job in a factory. Paula objects to the introduction of the form. What ruling?

4.12   In a consumer fraud action involving allegations of bait and switch, plaintiff seeks to introduce evidence that he went to the defendant's store during business hours. He said to the store owner, within hearing of several other customers, "You guys think your pretty smart. You advertise that cheap stuff and then never have it when the customer comes in." The defendant made no response. Is plaintiff's testimony admissible?

4.13   *Paula v. David and PDG.* David does not take the stand, nor does he offer any eyewitness testimony. Instead, David chooses to rely on accident reconstruction experts. In closing argument, Paula's attorney argues, "It seems strange that the defendant did not take the stand on his own behalf." Is this argument objectionable?

4.14   Consider: *Still admissible*

    .01   Assume in problem 4.10.06, that instead of the plaintiff signing the complaint, the complaint was signed by the plaintiff's lawyer. Is the complaint admissible?

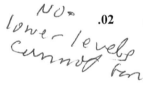
No — lower levels cannot bind State

    .02   *State v. Duffy.* Arlo seeks to call a newspaper reporter who will testify that Officer Gorham said during the investigation, "I never have thought Arlo was smart enough to pull off this job." Is the testimony admissible?

4.15   Plaintiff claims that a truck driver while on company business struck the plaintiff as she walked across a parking lot.

Yes — agent's statement, so admissible

    .01   Immediately upon hitting the plaintiff, the truck driver got out of the truck and said, "Gee, I'm sorry. I didn't see you." In the suit against the employer based on respondeat superior, may plaintiff testify to the driver's statement?

If in scope of empl. then admissible

    .02   Assume that instead of making the statement immediately after the accident, the driver visited the plaintiff in the hospital that evening and made the statement. Would there be a different result?

No authority

    .03   Assume that between the time the accident occurred, and the time the driver went to the hospital to make the statement, the employer fired the truck driver. Would that change your answer in 4.15.02?

firing admission?

    .04   Would the fact that the driver was fired on the day of the accident be admissible? Suppose at the time the truck driver was fired the employer said, "I'm tired of your

Y C S   carelessness, you're fired." Could the employee's statement be testified to by the driver?

4.16   In a wrongful death action, an airline is sued for negligence when a plane crashed on landing. Before the law suit was filed, an employee of the airline, an engineering test pilot, conducted an investigation of the accident. When contacted by the plaintiff after suit was filed, the employee wrote a letter to the plaintiff stating, "The consensus is that this was an unfortunate accident, just too short and low a landing." Defendant objects to the admissibility of this letter based on hearsay. Should the letter be excluded? Would your answer be different if the quoted statement were contained in an internal report resulting from an investigation authorized by the company and conducted by the employee? Would it make any difference if the pilot made the statement on the basis of only having talked to two eyewitnesses?

4.17   Plaintiff sues the owner of a grocery store for negligence in not mopping up a spill on the floor. Plaintiff alleges she slipped and fell on the spill and suffered great injury.   A clerk, seeing the plaintiff fall came up to her and said, "Sorry the floor was wet, I was just getting ready to mop it up." May plaintiff testify to the clerk's statement over an objection of hearsay? Assume it was the store manager that made the statement, what result?

4.18   Robert Chappell is charged with a scheme to defraud investors in an oil well. Criminal charges were filed after a Securities Exchange Commission (SEC) investigation.   At trial, the prosecutor seeks to introduce the transcript of the deposition of a former employee of Chappell's. The employee was the bookkeeper employed by Chappell during the time of the SEC investigation. The deposition was taken in conjunction with the SEC investigation. The bookkeeper left the company one year ago, but remains as bookkeeper in an independent contractor status. The former employee is available to testify. Is the deposition admissible?

4.19 Refer to problem 4.16. Assume the airline is the wholly owned subsidiary of a larger diversified corporation. Assume also that the letter came not from the airline company actually involved in the accident, but from the parent corporation of the airline. Under what circumstances, if any, should the letter be admissible by plaintiff?

4.20   Refer to problems 4.1.13 and 4.10.02. Suppose Al wins and is then sued by Oscar. Oscar claims that he, not Al, is the true owner of the gun. Oscar wishes to introduce the testimony of a neighbor of Al's now deceased father who will testify that Al's father said to the neighbor, "I took that sucker [meaning the antique gun] from Oscar's daddy and he didn't even know, ha ha." Al objects. What ruling?

4.21   Defendant is on trial for possession of drugs. Defendant was arrested with two other people when the Coast Guard boarded a boat based on probable cause to believe the defendant and the other two planned to smuggle drugs. The prosecutor seeks to introduce the testimony of a Coast Guard officer. The officer will testify that after he boarded the boat, but before he began to search, one of defendant's companions said, that the boat was a charter operation taking scuba divers out to the reef, and "we are all in this together." Defendant objects to the testimony on the basis of hearsay and the Sixth Amendment Confrontation Clause. What ruling? Does it make a difference whether the companion is unavailable? Assume the quoted portion of the statement was made after the drugs were found and during questioning in which the declarant admitted his guilt on drug charges. What result? Assume the statement was made in the presence of the defendant and that the defendant remained silent. What result?

yes (difference) - must be made in furtherance of the conspiracy

D. Spontaneous Declarations

4.22   Defendant, an air conditioning repair technician, is charged with murder. The prosecutor calls to the stand the husband of the victim who, if allowed, will testify that 30 minutes before his wife was found dead, he had talked to his wife on the phone and she had said,

present condition

.01   "I haven't been able to get to the store yet, since the guy is still here repairing the air conditioner."

.02   "I still can't get to the store, the air conditioning guy left fifteen minutes ago, I hope to get a part. At least I think he's coming back."

Is this testimony admissible over hearsay objections?

4.23   *Donato v. Donato.* Paul calls to the witness stand a neighbor of Gina's who will testify that she was walking past Gina's house when a person she had never seen before, but believes was a salesman, came out of the house and said, "What a pig sty. I can't believe people actually live in that mess." Is this testimony admissible over a hearsay objection?

4.24   Refer to problem 4.15. The truck driver after hitting the plaintiff got out of the truck and said, "I'm in big trouble now. My boss told me to get this load delivered by quitting time." May plaintiff testify over a hearsay objection that this statement was made?

4.25   Refer to problem 4.8. Forty-five minutes after the alleged rape, Alice was taken by her grandmother to the police. The prosecutor calls a police officer who, if allowed, will testify as follows:

Q: What did you do when the grandmother brought in the girl?

A: Well, the first thing I noticed was her clothes all torn and her face beginning to show some bruises, so I asked, "What happened?"

Q: How did Alice respond?

A: She immediately broke down and started to cry, but then kinda' between sobs she tells me that her Mommy's friend, the defendant there, tried to pull down her jeans, and tried to touch her places her mommy told her not to let people. When she fought and screamed, she said the defendant hit her.

Is this testimony admissible?

4.26   Danny is on trial for robbery of a liquor store. He is alleged to have robbed it with his friend Joe. Joe has already been convicted of the crime. Immediately after fleeing the scene of the crime, it is alleged that Danny and Joe went to Joe's girlfriend's house and partied through the night. At various times during the night Danny left the party. As the party was winding down, Joe started to count his money taken in the robbery and the girlfriend asked, "Where's Danny's share?" Joe replied, "He has already gone through all of his money." The prosecutor seeks to call the girlfriend to testify to this exchange with Joe. Defense counsel objects. What result?

4.27   Sarah, the owner of a wine distributorship, sues Betty, the owner of a wine shop, for breach of contract. Sarah claims that she and Betty contracted for the purchase of several cases of expensive French wine. Sarah claims her copy of the correspondence that forms the contract has been destroyed in a recent fire. Betty denies the existence of the contract. Is the following testimony hearsay, and if so, is it admissible under Federal Rule of Evidence 803(3) or its common law equivalent?

.01   Sarah will testify that in a letter from her to Betty she offered to sell the wine for $5,000, and that a letter in response stated that Betty would buy it for $4,000. Sarah then sent a letter saying she would sell the wine for $4,000.

.02   Sarah will call Warren, the owner of a different wine shop. Warren will testify that a day before Sarah allegedly sent her original letter to Betty, he was at Sarah's warehouse and offered to buy the wine. Sarah refused his offer, saying, "No, I want to see this in Betty's shop. Her customers will appreciate it."

.03   Suppose Warren will testify that just before Sarah sent the letter agreeing to the $4,000, Warren was at Sarah's warehouse. Warren saw the wine in question and offered to buy it. Sarah, however, refused to sell it, saying, "No, I'm going to sell that to your competitor, Betty, and I'm getting 4 grand."

Past conduct
can it be used

.04 Suppose Warren visited the warehouse after Sarah allegedly sent the letter accepting the $4,000 counter offer. When Warren asked to purchase the wine, Sarah said, "Sorry, you're too late. I've sold it to your competitor, Betty."

803.3
intent

4.28 Defendant is charged with extortion. The prosecutor claims the defendant came into possession of credit card invoices and then made extortionate demands for their return. Defendant seeks to introduce the testimony of his previous lawyer who will state that at some point prior to defendant's arrest he and the defendant discussed the legality of the defendant negotiating a reward for having found credit card invoices. Specifically, the lawyer will testify that the defendant said, "I intend to negotiate a reward. Is it legal?" Is the testimony admissible? Suppose, instead, the lawyer will testify that the defendant said, "Is it legal to negotiate for a reward for something you find?" Is this statement admissible? Would it make a difference what the lawyer said in response? Is what the lawyer said hearsay?

Hillmon
803(3)

4.29 Refer to problem 4.22. The victim's husband will testify as follows.

.01 "I spoke to Mary about 30 minutes before the neighbor found her dead. She called me from the store to tell me she was running home because she had to meet the air conditioner repairman."

past
shepard

.02 "I spoke with Mary about 30 minutes before the neighbor found her dead. She called me from home and said she had run home from the store to meet the repairman, but that he was late."

Defendant's attorney objects. What ruling?

on Wed 4/28/01

4.30 Refer to problem 4.8 and 4.25. After talking to the police, Alice was taken by the police and her grandmother to the hospital emergency room where she was seen by a physician, Dr. Harris. The prosecutor seeks to call Dr. Harris who, if allowed, will testify as follows:

803(4)

I came into the room and I asked Alice what happened. She did not answer. I asked her if she had any pain and she pointed to her vaginal area. I then asked her if she hurt anyplace else, but she did not answer. I asked again what happened and she said Doug had dragged her to her bedroom. I asked if he had taken off her clothes and she said yes. Then she said that he had tried to stick something into her vagina which hurt. She tried to scream, but was unable, because Doug had a hand over her mouth and neck.

.01 Is this testimony admissible under Federal Rule 803(4) over defense counsel's objection?

.02   Assume that Dr. Harris was unable to get any information from Alice, and turned to the police officer who had interviewed her in problem 4.25. The police officer then told Dr. Harris that on the car ride over, Alice had told him this information. May Dr. Harris testify over defense counsel's objection concerning what the police officer told him?

.03   Assume Dr. Harris is a psychiatrist. Also assume Alice is four years old, rather than nine, and was taken to Dr. Harris' office in a suburban building and introduced to Alice as a friend of Alice's grandmother. Is this testimony admissible under Federal Rule 803(4) over defense counsel's objection?

4.31   For each of the following indicate whether the evidence is hearsay, and, if so, whether it is admissible under an exception to the hearsay rule.

Adam Klare brought suit for medical malpractice against Donald Bradman, a physician. Bradman allegedly failed to come to the hospital when Adam needed his attention. Bradman is the only defendant. Bradman admitted Adam to the hospital for an operation to repair a broken leg. One night at the hospital, at approximately 3:00 a.m., Adam complained of pain in the leg and lack of feeling in his toes. The toes were cold and bluish in color. These were all indications that the cast was cutting off the circulation in his lower leg. The nurse assigned to Adam's room that night was Diane Loso. Bradman's defense is that he was never informed of the seriousness of the symptoms.

.01   Adam seeks to have his mother take the stand to testify that Adam called her at about 3:10 a.m. and told her, "My leg hurts something awful, and the doctors don't seem to care. It's turning bluer and bluer because the doctors won't take care of it. What should I do?" His mother will also testify that she called the hospital after talking to her son, and told the nurses that her son was in great pain.

.02   Adam seeks to call Diane Loso to testify that he (Adam) said at 3:00 a.m., "My leg started hurting an hour ago, and it hurts somethin' awful right now."

.03   Adam seeks to take the stand himself to testify that at approximately 3:20 a.m., nurse Loso came to his room and said, "Don't worry, I've spoken to Dr. Bradman, and he said that everything would be fine and that he'll see you in the morning."

.04   Bradman seeks to call a second nurse, Candice Krieling, to testify that Loso said at approximately 3:15 a.m., "I'm going to call Bradman. Klare's in there complaining again. It's always something with that guy."

.05   Joe Basanta was in the bed next to Adam on the night in question. Joe also had a broken leg. Six months after the night in question, Joe was in a car crash and suffered injuries which ultimately caused his death. Before he died, however, Joe was taken back to the same hospital in which the present malpractice is alleged to have occurred. As Joe lay dying in the same hospital with two severed legs caused by the car crash, the only words he said were, "Don't let them take me back to the same floor I was on before. Those nurses cost Adam his leg." Adam wishes to call Gene Basanta, Joe's father, who was present at the time Joe made this statement.

E. Records

4.32   Witness Examination. *State v. Duffy.* Officer Mundy is on the stand, has been sworn, and has testified as to what her job is.

    .01   She then testified that she had no present recollection of the robbery investigation. Lay the appropriate foundation to allow her to read from her police report dated June 1, Yr-0.

    .02   Assume she can remember, but is a bit unclear on certain details, lay the appropriate foundation.

4.33   Witness Examination. Refer to 4.32.01. Having laid the foundation, the following testimony occurred:

> By the prosecutor: Your honor, at this point I request State's Exhibit A For Identification be admitted into evidence as State's Exhibit A.

> By Defense Counsel: Objection your honor, hearsay.

    .01   State the correct ruling and reason.

> Q (By the prosecutor): Did you speak to the tellers?

> A: Yes.

> Q: Who were they?

> By Defense Counsel: Objection your honor, hearsay.

    .02   State the correct ruling and reason.

Q: Did the robber say anything to Van Donk?

A: Yes.

Q: What did he say?

By Defense Counsel: Objection your honor, hearsay.

.03   State the correct ruling and reason.

A: Keep quiet and hand me the money.

Q: Did he have anything in his hand?

By Defense Counsel: Objection your honor, hearsay.

.04   State the correct ruling and reason.

A: Yes.

Q: What was it?

A: A big gun.

Q: Did Ms. Van Donk describe the robber?

A: Yes.

Q: How did she describe him?

By Defense Counsel: Objection your honor, hearsay.

.05   State the correct ruling and reason.

A: White, male 5'9", about 160 pounds.

Q: Were there any other customers in the bank at the time of the robbery?

By Defense Counsel: Objection your honor, hearsay.

.06   State the correct ruling and reason.

4.34 Plaintiff brings suit alleging a slip and fall on defendant's property. Defendant claims the fall never occurred and that the injuries claimed are from an occurrence before the alleged slip and fall. Defendant wants to introduce a memo summarizing an interview of plaintiff. The interview, conducted by an employee of the defendant's insurance company, occurred immediately after the fall. In the interview, plaintiff mentioned the prior injury, but did not mention any present injury. The insurance company employee has no present recollection, but as a matter of regular business practice, prepares this kind of memo in every case he handles. Is the memo admissible?

4.35 Plaintiff moved across country and entrusted all his property to Harold Van Lines. Harold lost the property someplace in Iowa. Plaintiff wants to introduce the notebook in which he listed all the items he owned as they were loaded on the truck. What options are available for using the notebook?

4.36 Plaintiff sues defendant to collect $100 due on the sale of merchandise. Defendant claims she only bought $10 worth and has paid that amount. Plaintiff's records are all computerized and show the value of the merchandise was $100. Can plaintiff introduce the computer records? What form would they take?

4.37 *Paula v. David and PDG.* Two police officers investigate the accident. Police officer Able interviewed Wanda. Police officer Baker interviewed Walter. Wanda tells Able the light was green for Paula. Walter tells Baker the light was green for David. Baker measures skid marks and tells Able the measurements. Able puts all the above information in his report. When called to the stand by plaintiff, Able seeks to rely on his report and relate what Wanda, Walter and Baker said. Defendant objects based on hearsay. What ruling? Assume, Baker is on the stand, would that change the ruling?

4.38 Refer to problem 4.31.

  .01 Adam wishes to introduce a portion of the nurses notes, part of the hospital record, for the night in question that provides:

> 3:15 a.m. called Dr. B & informed him of bluish toes
> and cold and informed him about patient complaints of
> leg pain. Requested he come see patient. Dr. said call
> back in a.m. /s/ D. Loso, R.N.

  Is this record admissible over an objection of hearsay?

  .02 Bradman seeks to introduce a portion of the doctors' progress notes, part of the hospital record, for the day in question which provides:

> 7:30 a.m. Patient complaining of pain in the leg and numbness in toes. Toes are cold and bluish. Nurse should have insisted come in last night. Called to schedule surgery. /s/ Bradman, M.D.

Is this record admissible over an objection of hearsay?

.03   Nurse Loso, following Adam's complaint, and consistent with hospital policy, completed a document known as an incident report. This report, sent to the hospital's risk management committee, is designed to report objectively any life threatening incident so that the hospital can take steps to avoid having the incident, and potential harm, repeated. Adam seeks to introduce this document as a business record. What result? Assume Dr. Bradman seeks to introduce the report. What result? Regardless of whether the report is admissible under the hearsay rule, should it be excluded for any other reason?

4.39   Plaintiff, the manufacturer of vodka, sues the defendant, a shipper of bulk liquid. Plaintiff alleges that defendant failed to clean adequately the large stainless steel trailer tank used to ship a large quantity of vodka. Specifically, defendant is alleged to have failed to clean the tanker truck after delivery of a load of milk. On cross-examination of the defendant's president, the following took place.

Q: Isn't it true that the standard procedure of your company is to steam clean the tank after each use?

A: Yes.

Q: And isn't this especially important following a shipment of something that spoils, like milk?

A: Yes.

Q: And certainly its true that when you use the tank for one purpose, like milk, and then use it for another purpose, like vodka, you must clean the tank?

A: Yes.

Q: In fact, didn't you say in your deposition that your standard procedure for such cleaning is for the truck depot to conduct the cleaning, and then, as a routine matter, send a report, really just a form with check marks and a signature, to the main office?

A: Yes.

Q: You haven't introduced any of those forms in this trial have you?

By Defense Counsel: Objection, your honor, hearsay.

What is the correct ruling?

4.40 *Donato v. Donato.*

> **.01** **Witness Examination.** At the hearing to determine custody, Gina would like to introduce the following documents. For Gina, attempt to introduce the documents in whatever manner is appropriate. For Paul, oppose the introduction of the evidence. The Reed Street address is the tavern beneath Paul's apartment.

Police Department   Case Yr-1-5693
Complaint and Service Request Report

Nature of Complaint __Noise__   Location __999 Reed St.__
Complainant __anonymous__   Address _____
Received by __Sgt. Spire__   Time _1:15 p.m._
                                            Details

Complaint that noise from band was disturbing neighborhood. Went to tavern at above address and spoke to Matthew Vitti. Band is noisy, but did not appear excessive, given that location is Tavern and apparently zoned for this activity.
                                                                        8/9/Yr-1

Approved by	Investigated by	Date

Police Department   Case Yr-0-345
Complaint and Service Request Report
Nature of Complaint __drunk__   Location __999 Reed St.__
Complainant __unknown__   Address _____
Received by __Sgt. James__   Time _1:00 p.m._
                                            Details
Phone call that there was fight at bar located this address. Officer arrived and saw two men arguing on street. Officer told both to move along and be quiet. No evidence of violence, and neither man indicated needed help. No further action taken.

                                                                        1/26/Yr-0

Approved by	Investigated by	Date

Police Department   Case Yr-1-3990
Complaint and Service Request Report

Nature of Complaint ___drunk___   Location ___999 Reed St.___
Complainant   ___anonymous___   Address _____
Received by   ___Sgt. Spire___   Time   ___11:05 p.m.___
                                          Details

Drunk from tavern at above address was sleeping on sidewalk. Told to move. Became obnoxious, taken to station, released to wife. No other action taken.

                                                                6/3/Yr-1

Approved by   Investigated by   Date

> **.02**   Paul seeks to introduce testimony of a private investigator who, if allowed will testify that he did a thorough search of records of the City Department of Licenses and Inspections and found no record of any housing code violations for the apartment in which Paul lives.

4.41   State v. Duffy. Officer Gorham is unavailable for trial. Under Federal Rule of Evidence 803(8), may the prosecutor offer a certified copy of Officer Gorham's report, instead of calling him to testify? Could the report be introduced by the records clerk of the police station where Officer Gorham is assigned? Is there any other way in which the document could be used?

4.42   Defendant, Simontov Yakobov, a.k.a. Yakov Yokubov, is charged with conspiracy to violate, and actual violation of, federal firearms statutes. It is alleged that he sold and shipped goods to Northern Ireland without an appropriate license.

> **.01**   The prosecutor seeks to introduce certified copies of records of the Royal Ulster Constabulary to show that weapons containing specified serial numbers were found in Northern Ireland. Defendant objects. What ruling?

> **.02**   To prove the defendant was not licensed by the federal government to export weapons, the prosecutor offers the signed, sworn, statement of the regional director of the Treasury Department's Bureau of Alcohol, Tobacco and Firearms (ATF). ATF is the appropriate licensing body. The statement provided:

> Being duly sworn, I hereby certify that after a diligent search of
> the records in my control, I found no license issued to Simontov
> Yakobov which would authorize the sale and export of firearms.

Defendant objects. What ruling?

4.43   A Navy flight instructor was killed when her airplane, 3E955, crashed during a training flight. A Navy officer made the service's official investigation of the accident. This "JAG Report" made the following findings:

> At approximately 1020, while turning crosswind without proper interval between
> other aircraft, 3E955 crashed, immediately caught fire and burned. At the time of
> the impact, the engine of 3E955 was operating, but at reduced power.

> Due to the death of the pilot and the destruction of the plane, it is almost impossible
> to determine exactly what happened, but the most probable cause of the accident
> was the pilot's failure to maintain a proper interval between planes, causing the
> pilot to take an abrupt avoidance maneuver during which the plane stalled and then
> crashed.

> Although the above sequence of events is the most likely to have occurred, it does
> not change the possibility that the crash was caused by a defect in the fuel control
> unit resulting in loss of power sufficient to conduct the avoidance maneuver.

At trial, plaintiff, husband of the dead pilot, seeks to introduce the JAG Report against defendant, the manufacturer of the airplane. Defendant's counsel objects based on hearsay. What ruling?

F. Additional Exceptions

4.44   Refer to problem 4.31. Adam seeks, in his case-in-chief, to introduce a textbook that during a deposition Bradman recognized as authoritative. The relevant portion states:

> One of the clearest symptoms that a leg has been casted too tightly is the loss of
> feeling resulting from decreased circulation.

4.45   *Paula v. David and PDG.* Prior to trial, David was convicted of driving under the influence at the time of the accident, a misdemeanor. He was sentenced to a weekend in jail and had his license suspended. Paula seeks to have the record of conviction admitted into evidence in her lawsuit against David and PDG. Is the record admissible? Assume that David's truck, after hitting Paula, ran up a sidewalk striking Harriet. Harriet died and David was tried and convicted of negligent homicide. David received an 18 month suspended sentence. Is this record of conviction admissible in the subsequent civil action? Does it matter that the evidence will also be used against PDG?

4.46   Plaintiff seeks to establish the value of her property by showing the value of comparable properties. To establish the value of comparable properties, plaintiff seeks to introduce the "Guide to Real Estate," a monthly publication produced by local real estate agencies, showing residential properties for sale in the metropolitan area. Defendant objects. What ruling?

4.47   Plaintiff brings suit on a life insurance policy, claiming he is entitled to double indemnity, because of the accidental death of the insured. The insurance company seeks to introduce a certified copy of the insured's death certificate. It is stated on the certificate that death was the result of a heart attack. Plaintiff objects. What ruling?

4.48   The United States brought an action seeking to obtain possession of a bell recovered from the C.S.S. Alabama, a Confederate commerce raider sunk by the Union Navy off the coast of Cherbourg, France in 1864. The United States claims the right to possession either by right of succession to all property of the former Confederate States of America or by right of capture. Appellant Richard Steinmetz bought the bell in England in 1979 and brought it back to the United States. When he put it up for auction in 1990, the United States Navy claimed that the bell was its property. How will the Navy's attorney establish the historical facts of this case?

G. Preliminary Review

4.49   **Motion In Limine.** *State v. Duffy.* Trial is scheduled for next week. The judge has called a pretrial conference at which, among other things, she will entertain motions in limine. Prepare the arguments and oral motions you will make concerning the following evidence. Prepare to represent both the defendant and the state. **Be sure to fill out the questionnaire following your preparation.**

> .01   Assuming Arlo does not admit the briefcase is his, on the issue of whether Arlo owns the brief case, the arresting police officer proposes to testify that Arlo said, when confronted with the case, "Hey, where did you find that?"

> .02   On the issue of whether Arlo was the robber, the investigating police officer proposes to testify describing the clothes the robber was reportedly wearing at the time of the crime.

> .03   Assume Arlo Duffy was convicted and another defendant, alleged to have helped

Arlo rob the bank, is now on trial. A bank teller with firsthand knowledge wishes to testify that Arlo Duffy said, "Give me the money or you're dead."

.04 Assume the evidence is conflicting on the issue of whether the robber was armed at the time of the robbery. One teller testifies that while the robber was at the window of another teller, the other teller fell over from what later turned out to be a fatal heart attack. Just before she collapsed of the heart attack, the teller said, "Oh no! He's got a gun!"

.05 On the issue of how much money was taken from the bank, the prosecutor seeks to introduce the deposit and withdrawal slips for all customers of the bank on the day of the robbery.

H. Unavailability Required

Yes - 804(b)(1)

4.50 Parker was driving his car at the intersection of Libbie and Grove, with his passenger Rachael, when there was a collision with Dan. The accident was witnessed by Walter. Parker sued Dan, calling Walter as a witness. Walter testified that Parker had the green light. The jury returned a verdict for Parker. Having seen that Parker was successful, Rachael brought suit against Dan. Between the judgment for Parker and the filing of Rachael's lawsuit, however, Walter died. In the subsequent lawsuit, may Rachael introduce that part of the transcript from the previous trial containing Walter's testimony?

Yes - but similar motive

4.51 Refer to problem 4.50. Assume instead that Parker and Rachael jointly bring suit against Dan. Walter is called to testify on behalf of plaintiffs, but the jury returns a verdict for Dan. Rachael then sues Parker. In the interim, Walter has been convicted of a felony and is serving time in a different state. In the second civil lawsuit, may Rachael introduce that part of the transcript from the previous trial containing Walter's testimony?

No - unless Rachel shown to be predecessor in interest

4.52 Refer to problem 4.50. Assume, however, that Dan calls Walter and he testifies that Dan had the green light. The jury, however, still returns a verdict against Dan. Rachael, the passenger, then brings suit against Dan. Dan again calls Walter to testify, but Walter refuses to testify. The court holds Walter in contempt. In the subsequent lawsuit, may Dan introduce that part of the transcript from the previous trial containing Walter's testimony?

4.53 Refer to problem 4.31. Bradman seeks to introduce the deposition of Harold Kellogg, a third nurse who was working the night in question. Harold testified as follows at a deposition:

I was the charge nurse that evening and Diane Loso would have checked with me before she called Dr. Bradman. I just don't remember her saying anything about Bradman saying he wouldn't come in. I'm not even sure she asked him to come in.

Harold has subsequently moved out of state and resides across country, he is unavailable at trial. Is the deposition admissible?

4.54   Assume, for the purposes of this question that the deposition referred to in the previous problem was introduced. Assume also that Adam's attorney recently sent an investigator to re-interview Harold at his new home. During that interview Harold was shown the medical records referred to in question 4.38 and he said,

> I wasn't sure at the deposition, but that was before I'd had a chance to look at these medical records. Now it all comes back, again, I don't know what Bradman said to her, but I do remember Diane saying the toes felt cold. I'm not sure about the pain or the bluishness, but definitely the cold.

May the investigator testify as to Harold's statement?

4.55   Peter was injured when a hole ripped open in the commercial airliner he was flying in on a trip to Hawaii. Peter brought suit against the airline alleging that a member of the ground crew failed to latch properly the cargo doors, causing the door to open during flight. Peter's deposition was taken by the airline.

> **.01**   Prior to trial, Peter died from his injuries. Would Peter's deposition be admissible even though the lawsuit now involves wrongful death?

> **.02**   Assume Peter's suit is settled, Peter dies, and another passenger brings a lawsuit based on the same incident. Is Peter's deposition admissible by the plaintiff in the subsequent lawsuit? Now, assume that in the subsequent lawsuit the plaintiff sues not only the airline, as Peter did, but has sues the manufacturer of the airplane on a products liability theory. Is Peter's deposition admissible?

4.56   Anthony is charged with fraud and racketeering.

> **.01**   At his preliminary hearing on the criminal charges, Anthony's lawyer, following a common practice among defense attorneys, chooses not to cross-examine the arresting police officer. After the preliminary hearing, but before trial, the police officer dies. May the prosecutor introduce the transcript of the officer's testimony from the preliminary hearing?

> **.02**   Bruno, an alleged co-conspirator, testified at the grand jury, under a grant of

immunity. At the grand jury, Bruno testified that neither he nor the defendant were involved in any scheme to defraud, nor were they engaged in racketeering. At trial, Anthony calls Bruno, hoping that Bruno will provide the same exculpatory testimony. Bruno, however, invokes his Fifth Amendment privilege against self-incrimination and refuses to testify. Anthony now seeks to introduce a transcript of Bruno's grand jury testimony. The prosecutor objects. What ruling?

.03 In the previous problem assume instead that at the grand jury Bruno admitted his own guilt and implicated Anthony in the illegal activity as well. At trial, the prosecution calls Bruno expecting him to provide the same testimony. Bruno, however, invokes his Fifth Amendment privilege against self-incrimination and refuses to testify. The prosecutor now seeks to introduce a transcript of Bruno's grand jury testimony. Defense counsel objects. What ruling?

4.57 Colonel Wharton is on trial for manslaughter. The facts as alleged by the prosecutor are that Colonel Wharton deliberately drove his car head-on into an oncoming semi-tractor trailer truck resulting in his wife's death. The prosecutor seeks to introduce the testimony of a nurse who cared for Mrs. Wharton following the incident. If allowed, the nurse will testify that after being told by the doctor that she was dying from internal injuries caused by the accident, Mrs. Wharton indicated a need to talk to someone. When the nurse said she would listen, Mrs. Wharton said:

> Colonel Wharton put the accelerator on the floorboard and turned the car deliberately head-on into the tractor-trailer. He did it on purpose. He asked me if I wanted to go to eternity with him. This collision was not an accident. He said "we will go to eternity together."

Yes

.01 Is the nurse's testimony admissible? Would it make a difference if Mrs. Wharton did not die, but had slipped into a coma and Mr. Wharton was on trial for attempted murder? *＼ no*

common law

No **.02** Assume Colonel Wharton was convicted of manslaughter. He then committed
yes-federal suicide. United Services Automobile Association (USAA), an insurer, brought a declaratory judgment action against the administrator of the estate of Colonel Wharton. USAA seeks a declaration of its obligations under a policy issued to Colonel Wharton covering his automobile. The policy specifically excludes coverage of intentional torts. Is Mrs. Wharton's statement admissible in this action?

Common law **.03** Assume that in addition to Mrs. Wharton, the driver of the tractor-trailer also died
had to be victim and Colonel Wharton is on trial for manslaughter in the death of the driver. Is the nurse's testimony admissible.

.04 Assume Mrs. Wharton lived and Colonel Wharton died. USAA refused to pay benefits under the insurance policy and Mrs. Wharton brings suit. May USAA

Under fed rules - Yes
common law, no civil

introduce the testimony a passenger in the car who will testify that just before the collision Colonel Wharton said "we will go to eternity together."

4.58   Paul brings an action to quiet title to a piece of real estate. Paul claims he has valid record title, having received it by intestate succession upon the death of his father, Grant. Grant was in actual possession of the property for 5 years, until his death one year ago. Paul has been in possession of the property since his father's death. Denny claims he is the rightful owner under a valid deed. Are the following statements admissible?

> **.01**   Denny seeks to call a witness, Wayne, to testify that three years ago he went to Grant and offered to buy the property. Wayne will testify that Grant said, "I'd love to sell it to you, but I'm only renting."

> **.02**   Denny also seeks to call Walter who will testify that two years ago he was hunting on the property and Grant told him to get off. When Walter said he had the owner's permission, Grant said, "I don't care who you talked to, I rent this place and I want you off."

4.59   Andrea, a nurse, is charged with murder in the deaths of several patients at a hospital. After Andrea is arrested, Beverly, the head nurse who supervised Andrea is diagnosed as having cancer, and on her death bed says, "I can't go to my death with this on my conscious. I killed those patients, not Andrea." Before trial, Beverly dies. May Andrea introduce Beverly's statement? Suppose the statement had been, "Andrea and I felt so sorry for those patients, we just had to end their misery." Is the statement admissible by the prosecutor? Suppose the statement were, "I eased the way for the first three patients by myself, Andrea was on her own for the last four." Admissible?

4.60   *Paula v. David and PDG.* Paula has a sworn statement from the mechanic who repaired her car following the accident. Before trial, the mechanic died. To prove both the extent of her injuries as well as the extent of damage to her car, Paula seeks to introduce the sworn statement. Should such a statement be admissible under 804(b)(5)?

I. Constitutional Concerns

4.61   Defendant is charged with receiving stolen property. To prove the car was stolen, the prosecutor seeks to introduce the felony conviction of the person who allegedly transferred the car to the defendant. The conviction is for stealing the car in question. Defense counsel objects. What ruling? Suppose that as a matter of substantive criminal law the prosecutor must show the conviction of the thief in order to obtain a conviction of the receiver. Would this affect your answer?

4.62 In problem 4.8 the prosecutor wishes to introduce the testimony of a psychiatric social worker who has been counseling Alice since the attempted rape. If permitted, the social worker will testify that three months after the incident, Alice told her that Doug had on several occasions tried to pull down her jeans, and touch her places her mommy told her not to let people touch. When she fought and screamed, she said Doug would hit her. Defense counsel objects based on hearsay and the Sixth Amendment Confrontation Clause. What ruling? Would it make a difference that Alice herself will not testify? Would it matter if the testimony referred to in problem 4.25 had been admitted?

4.63 Refer to problem 4.31. Assume, however, the suit is against the hospital. Also assume Adam never called his mother during the night. At approximately 4:00 a.m. the morning in question, Nurse Loso was in the room adjacent to Adam's. She testified that she heard a loud thump against the wall in Adam's room and immediately left to investigate. She discovered Adam on the floor and asked him what had happened. Based on what Adam told her and her personal observations, she made the following notation on Adam's clinical record:

> Found pt [patient] on floor--Apparently crawled out end of bed— trying to get to BR [bathroom]—had called for help but not a quick enough response.

Approximately eleven hours after Adam's fall, his parents arrived at the hospital unaware of the previous night's events. After learning from the station nurse that Adam had fallen, the Klares went to their son in his hospital room and asked him what had happened. Over the hospital's objection, Mrs. Klare testified as follows:

Q: Then what happened?

A: We ran into the room and we said, "Adam, what in the world's happened?" And he said, "Oh, Mother, it was terrible."

Q: What else did he say?

A: He said, "I put the call bell on," or the call light. He said, "I put the call bell on and I waited and I waited and no one came. I waited again and put the call bell on again two or three times." He'd keep punching it he said. "And no one came to help me. And I called out, 'help! Help me!' and no one came."

Q: Did he tell you how he managed to actually get someone to come?

A: He showed me that he got out through the rails, the split rails. He was smaller than he is now. He told me, he said, "I got out through these rails, Mother. And I fell. I hit my head and I hit my leg." And he said, "The nurse came in finally when I fell and she was mad at me. She bawled me out."

Klare's attorney then showed her Nurse Loso's notations on the clinical record, and asked her, through a series of questions, if the notations confirmed what Adam told her that next morning. Mrs. Klare testified that the two were consistent. There was additional testimony directly on the question of whether the hospital's response was tardy. Mrs. Klare testified that a couple of days after the incident in question:

> Nurse Loso came up in the hall, my husband and I were standing in the hall, and by Adam's room, and she said--she was crying and she said, "Mr. and Mrs. Klare, I am so sorry. I just couldn't get to Adam. I was with another patient. We're so short-handed and I was with another patient and I couldn't get to Adam. The call light was on and I heard him call, but I couldn't get to him." Nurse Loso, on direct examination, admitted apologizing to the Klares but denied ever telling them that the hospital was short-staffed or that she had heard the call bell. On cross-examination, Klare's attorney brought out that in a deposition taken a year earlier, Nurse Loso stated that she did not remember exactly what she had told the Klares.

Was the court correct in permitting Mrs. Klare's testimony?

4.64   Refer to problem 4.8. Arlo objects to the introduction of the testimony under 801(d)(1)(C) claiming a violation of his Sixth Amendment Confrontation Clause rights. What result?

CHAPTER 5

LAY AND EXPERT OPINIONS

5.1   Is any of the following permissible testimony?

    .01   *Paula v. David and PDG.* Walter seeks to testify that he was standing beside the road when,

        .A   "I heard this car zoom behind me on the cross street. It had to be going at least 60."

        .B   "I heard Paula's car speeding down the road."

        .C   "I saw Paula's car speeding down the road."

        .D   "I saw Paula's car coming about 60 miles per hour down the road."

    .02   *Donato v. Donato.* Mrs. Donato seeks to testify that, "Paul's apartment is a pig sty. He never cleans it up, and it's got roaches."

    .03   *Donato v. Donato.* Gina will testify, "Paul's apartment is simply too rundown for children. And worse, the neighborhood is simply dangerous."

    .04   A customs inspector wishes to testify that he suspected the defendant was illegally importing food because the inspector could smell "oranges."

    .05   *State v. Duffy.* Arlo raises as a defense that he was taking medication at the time of the robbery and that this medication made him psychotic, thus reducing his criminal liability. Sherry Van Donk will testify that "Arlo looked calm and collected. He certainly didn't look insane or crazy or anything like that."

    .06   *State v. Duffy.* Glenda Berg seeks to testify that Sherry Van Donk, when approached by the robber, "looked like she was very scared."

    .07   *Paula v. David and PDG.* Wanda seeks to testify that at the time of the accident David looked drunk. Assume the judge allows the testimony, what type of questions would you ask on cross-examination?

.08   ***State v. Duffy.*** Sherry Van Donk will testify that the photograph of the robber taken from the surveillance camera in the bank looks just like the defendant, Arlo Duffy.

.09   On the issue of why her husband was depressed, a wife seeks to testify that it was because he failed to receive a promotion at work and that this was part of a pattern of what she felt he believed were recent personal failures on his part.

.10   Plaintiff alleges that while she was driving her car, she was struck head-on by defendant who was driving a truck. On direct examination, defendant testifies that he was lawfully driving when an eight-year-old darted between parked cars, causing him to swerve to avoid hitting the child. As a result, he did strike plaintiff's car. He is then asked,

Q: If you had not swerved, would you have hit the child?

A: Yes.

Q: You have heard testimony concerning the plaintiff's injuries?

A: Yes.

Q: If you had not swerved to avoid hitting the child, would you have caused more damage to the child than was suffered by plaintiff?

A: The child would have died.

Assume the plaintiff makes timely objection to this testimony. How should the judge rule?

5.2   Witness Interview. *Donato v. Donato.* You represent Gina. You would like to have testimony concerning Gina's ability as a mother. You think Gina's own mother/father might make a good witness. Interview Gina's mother/father to determine whether she/he can and should testify as to Gina's fitness as a parent. **Your instructor will provide the person playing the father/mother with confidential information. Be sure to fill out the joint questionnaire following the simulation.**

5.3   Witness Examination. Using the information obtained in 5.2, conduct the direct examination of Gina's mother/father. Your instructor will provide you with additional information if you did not do 5.2.

5.4   Which of the following are proper subjects for expert testimony? In any of the cases, should expert testimony be required?

.01   In a medical malpractice action, plaintiff proposes to have a physician testify that it is improper medical procedure to leave a surgical sponge in a patient following an operation.

.02   In a criminal prosecution for violation of gambling laws, the prosecutor seeks to have testimony concerning how a bookmaking operation is conducted, including the language used by people involved in such an operation.

.03   *State v. Duffy.* Assume Sherry Van Donk can make a positive identification. In defense, Arlo calls a psychologist to the stand to testify concerning the inherent weakness of eyewitness identification, especially when a weapon is involved.

.04   In a personal injury action, plaintiff, an 18 year-old quadriplegic, seeks to introduce the testimony of an economist concerning his potential earnings had he not been injured.

.05   In an action to quiet title, plaintiff seeks to have a law professor testify that, according to the law of the jurisdiction, a properly conducted title search would have placed defendant on inquiry notice that plaintiff had superior title at the time defendant acquired his deed.

.06   In an action for attorney's fees following a successful civil rights law suit, counsel seeks to call an attorney who will testify that she has read the entire record in the case and in her opinion the fee requested is a reasonable attorney's fee.

.07   Refer to problem 5.1.08. Assume the photograph is unclear. The prosecutor calls an expert to make a comparison of the bone structure of the defendant with the bone structure of the person in the photograph. If allowed, the expert will then identify the defendant as the person in the photograph.

.08   Plaintiff, in a personal injury action arising out of an airplane crash, seeks to call a psychologist who has studied the survivors of airplane disasters and who will testify to the psychological stress the passengers experience when it becomes apparent that the plane will crash.

.09   In a criminal prosecution for assault and attempted rape of a six-year-old, the defendant testifies in his own behalf. In rebuttal the prosecutor seeks to have a psychologist testify that the defendant is a compulsive liar.

.10   In the previous question, suppose the prosecutor seeks to have the psychologist testify that the victim, who has already testified, knows the difference between telling the truth and lying.

5.5   In an action for violation of state obscenity laws, the legal standard requires applying contemporary community standards. Defendant seeks to introduce the testimony of a professional pollster who conducted a survey among 1400 households in the city in which the trial is taking place. Seventy-five percent of all respondents did not find the material obscene. The prosecutor objects. What ruling?

5.6   Which of the following involve a proper expert testifying about a proper subject matter?

.01   Mr. Perry brings a medical malpractice action arising out of treatment begun in an emergency room. Perry, alleges that Dr. Duke mistreated a chain saw cut to his knee by failing to read a lab report within 24 hours of the injury and by thereafter providing improper antibiotic treatment. Both actions, he claims, caused him to develop degenerative arthritis in his knee. Perry calls to the stand an emergency room staff nurse who will testify that 1) hospital policy requires lab reports of this kind be completed and returned to the patient's record within 24 hours, 2) the particular lab report in question was returned within 24 hours and 3) the doctor did not meet the accepted standard of care when he failed to read the report in a timely manner.

.02   In 5.6.01, defendant takes the witness stand to testify that the cause of plaintiff's continuing injury is not a failure to read a lab report. Rather, the cause of Perry's degenerative arthritis was the chain saw cutting into his knee.

.03   In problem 4.43 involving the crash of the Navy airplane, plaintiff, the spouse of the victim, seeks to testify. Plaintiff, himself is a navy pilot, but has never flown the type of plane involved in the crash. Having reviewed the investigation information, he will testify that in his opinion the crash was caused by a defective fuel mechanism resulting in a loss of power.

.04   In a criminal prosecution for sale of cocaine, the prosecutor offers the testimony of an FBI agent. The FBI agent has received training in drug identification based on appearance. He has been confirmed in his identifications on many occasions and seeks to testify that the drug sold was cocaine.

.05   Refer to the previous problem. Assume instead of the FBI agent, the prosecutor calls the buyer who will testify that he has been addicted to cocaine for five years and that he recognized the substance as cocaine.

.06   Landlord, the owner of 500 apartment units, sued a tenant for breach of the lease agreement, contending that the tenant had committed $3,000 worth of damage to the apartment. The landlord seeks to testify as to the cost of the damage to the property.

.07   Plaintiff, a cattle rancher, sues the defendant, a feed supplier, for negligence in preparing feed for plaintiff's cattle. Plaintiff calls as a witness his neighbor, also a rancher. The neighbor will testify that he has been a cattle rancher for 40 years. He started working soon after he dropped out of high school, and, except for a short time while in the military, has worked on cattle ranches ever since. He will state that, based on his examination of plaintiff's cattle, the cause of their illness is contaminated feed.

.08   Plaintiff, 16 years old, was paralyzed when he dived into defendant's pool. Defendant is a private club. In an action against the club, defendant seeks to introduce the testimony of an experienced swim instructor and high school teacher who will testify to the effect that teenagers have a propensity to be reckless around a swimming pool, and not pay attention when diving into the pool.

5.7   *State v. Duffy*. To support his alibi defense, Arlo introduced a photograph of himself and his mother which he says was taken on the day of the bank robbery. To establish the falsity of Arlo's alibi, the prosecutor, over objection, introduced the testimony of an astronomer who said that the photograph offered by Arlo could not have been taken on the day of the robbery. On appeal, Arlo challenges the admissibility of the astronomer's testimony. The following quotation is taken from the trial court's written opinion:

Defendant's motion involves the admission of a novel application of mathematical and astronomical theories of Dr. Ciupik. Ciupik testified that he was an associate astronomer at the Adler Planetarium in Chicago, working chiefly as the Observatory Director; he had authored two children's books on astronomy, worked as a consultant for Rand, McNally, and written articles for McGraw-Hill's Yearbook of Science and Technology. He had taught astronomy to gifted high school students, and was a member of a local professional organization. He was accepted by the court, without objection, as an expert capable of making astronomical calculations. Ciupik testified that as it revolves around the sun, the earth is fixed in its orientation towards the North Star. The sun's path as we perceive it in the daytime sky therefore repeats itself from year to year. Twice a year, on dates equidistant from the summer or winter solstices, the sun will be in precisely the same location with respect to both the horizon and the North Star. Ciupik then expounded the theory that if one knew the compass orientation of an object in a photograph, it would be possible to date that photograph by: 1) measuring the directional angle of the shadow cast by that object to determine the azimuth of the sun (the azimuth of the sun is its angle from true south); and 2) measuring the angle of elevation of a complete shadow cast by another object in the photograph to determine the altitude of the sun (the altitude of the sun is the angle formed by its elevation about the horizon). Ciupik stated that the intersection point of the altitude and the azimuth, defining the sun's position in the sky, corresponds to the only two dates of the year on which the photo could have been taken.

Ciupik further testified that he could determine those two dates by entering his finding for altitude and azimuth on a "sun chart." Although Ciupik could not ascertain who prepared the chart, or even under whose supervision it had been prepared some fifteen years ago, he testified that he had verified its accuracy with an Analog Computer and through continued usage. He stated, however, that the lines on the chart corresponding to the sun's path in the daytime sky were based on the sun's path on the 22nd day of each month, and that one would be compelled to interpolate the data obtained through his reverse calculations in order to determine the sun's position on any other day. Moreover, the only purpose for which the chart had been used in the past was to measure the height of lunar mountains. The chart, a pivotal piece of evidence, was admitted over objection that it was unverified hearsay, and therefore formed an inadequate basis for Ciupik's calculations. On cross-examination, Ciupik admitted that although he had made numerous measurements of lunar mountains with the aid of the chart, neither he nor anyone else as far as he knew had ever used it prior to this trial for the purpose of dating a photograph. Nor could he point to any published text suggesting or detailing the method one would use for such calculations.

How should the appellate court rule? What might the prosecutor or astronomer have done to increase the likelihood that the trial court's decision would be upheld?

5.8   ***Donato v. Donato.*** Paul claims Gina abuses the children. Paul, therefore, seeks to introduce expert testimony about the general characteristics of the battered child syndrome (BCS). BCS has previously been described by this expert as follows:

BCS indicates that a child of tender years found with a certain type of injury has not suffered those injuries by accidental means, but rather is the victim of child abuse. The diagnosis is used in connection with very young children, usually four years of age or younger, who cannot testify themselves. It is based upon a finding that such child exhibits evidence of, among other things, subdural hematoma, fractures in various stages of healing, soft tissue swelling or skin bruising. Also pertinent to the diagnosis is evidence that the child is generally undernourished and that the severity of injuries on his body is inconsistent with the parents' story of their occurrence.

In addition, the expert seeks to testify that Ellen exhibits symptoms consistent with the syndrome, and he therefore believes that she has been abused. In deciding whether this testimony should be admitted, what factors should the court take into consideration? Would it make a difference if the expert was to testify that the defendant had characteristics of a child abuser?

5.9   In a lawsuit involving the question of whether a mentally retarded child was receiving a federally mandated appropriate education, the parents seek to call a special education expert to testify. Reproduced below is the expert's resume. How might you use this resume to qualify the person as an expert?

RESUME

Samantha Tucker
90 Elm Street
Calhoun, Columbia

Education

Ph.D.   University of Michigan, Ann Arbor, Michigan
                    Educational Psychology/Special Education, Yr-5.

M.Ed.   University of California at Los Angeles.
                    Special Education, Yr-10.

B.A.   University of Richmond, Richmond, Virginia
                    Psychology, Yr-17.

Employment

Yr-5 to present   Assistant Superintendent, Special Education, York, New Hampshire.

Yr-10 - Yr-7   Director, Steele School, a private residential school for children with
                  severe emotional disabilities. Dover, Mass.

Yr-14 - Yr-12   Principal, Harris Special Education Center, public school for children
                  with wide range of physical and mental disabilities. Harris, N.Y.

Yr-12 - Yr-17   Teacher, Special Education, Harris Special Education Center, Harris,
                  N.Y.

Other Professional Experience

Adjunct Faculty, York Community College.
Consultant, York Association for Retarded Citizens.
Consultant/Expert Witness Special Education Litigation.

Professional Affiliations

Council for Exceptional Children (Board of Directors Yr-5 to present); American
Association on Mental Deficiency; National Association for Retarded Citizens.

Publications

"Special Education Centers and Their Conflict With Mainstreaming"; "Educational
Programming and the Severely Retarded"; "Parents, Schools and Conflicts Over
Education."

5.10   Refer to problem 5.6.01 and assume the plaintiff calls Dr. Edmonds. He testifies as follows:

Q: Dr. Edmonds, are you familiar with Mr. Perry?

A: Well, I've never met the gentleman, but I have reviewed his medical records.

Q: Which medical records?

A: I reviewed all the records of the emergency room where Mr. Perry went on the day of his injury. Then I obtained copies of his medical records from his present treating physician, Dr. Williams.

Q: Do you have information concerning Mr. Perry from any other source?

A: Yes. I had quite a long conversation with Dr. Williams concerning his treatment of Mr. Perry.

Q: Did these records indicate whether Mr. Perry was suffering from any permanent damage to his knee?

Defense Counsel: I object, your honor, this is hearsay.

Court: Overruled.

A: Yes, there was a reduction of mobility in the knee.

Q: Now, you indicated that you spoke to Dr. Williams. Specifically, what did he tell you?

Defense Counsel: Objection, your honor, hearsay.

Court: Objection sustained.

Q: Based on your review of these records, do you have an opinion as to the cause of the damage to the knee?

A: Yes.

Q: Is that opinion consistent with Dr. Williams' opinion?

Defense Counsel: Objection, your honor, hearsay.

Court: Objection sustained.

Were the court's rulings correct?

5.11   ***Paula v. David and PDG.*** Paula calls to the stand, Harold Hughes, Ph.D., an "accident reconstruction expert."

>   **.01**   After testifying to his qualifications, the court qualifies him as an expert. Paula then asks:
>
>>   Q: Do you have an opinion as to the cause of the accident?
>>
>>   Defense Counsel: I object your honor. There is no basis for this witness to give an expert opinion.
>
>   How should the judge rule?
>
>   **.02**   Assume the judge overrules the objection and the witness proceeds to give his opinion and nothing more. On cross-examination, the following occurs:
>
>>   Q: Dr. Hughes, isn't it true that you base your testimony on a limited number of different types of information?
>>
>>   A: I'm not sure I would agree.
>>
>>   Q: In fact, the information supporting your conclusion is based entirely on what other people have told you?
>>
>>   A: Not entirely. As I've testified, I have years of experience in this area.
>>
>>   Q: But you did not see this accident yourself?
>>
>>   A: No I didn't.
>>
>>   Q: In fact, would it be fair to say that you received most of your information from questioning bystanders and the plaintiff?
>>
>>   A: Yes, that would be a fair statement.
>
>   At this point, what should defense counsel do? If defense counsel was prepared to conduct this line of questioning on cross-examination, was there anything she could have done on direct examination?

5.12   Refer to problem 5.6.01. Having qualified Dr. Williams, Mr. Perry's treating physician as an expert, prepare the shortest possible direct examination in which he will testify to the causal connection between the failure to read the lab report and Mr. Perry's permanent leg disability.

5.13   In the previous problem, would Dr. Williams be able to testify, "In my opinion, Dr. Duke committed malpractice"? Would he be able to testify that, "In my opinion, Dr. Duke's treatment of Mr. Perry fell below the standard of acceptable medical practice within this state"? Would he be able to testify, "In my opinion acceptable medical practice would be to have read the lab report within 24 hours, and then administer intravenous antibiotics. This would have stopped the infection and there would have been no loss of mobility in the leg"?

5.14   In a criminal prosecution for first degree murder, defendant calls to the stand a psychiatrist who, if allowed, will testify, "In my opinion, the defendant's addiction to the drugs that were prescribed for him put him in such a cycle of depression that he was unable to take any premeditated action." Is this testimony objectionable?

5.15   **Witness Examination.** *Donato v. Donato.* Paul offers as a witness the Reverend Anthony Lonagoni, Jesuit Priest at St. Rita's, the church the Donato's attend. A summary of the Father's deposition follows:

> I am a 62 year old Jesuit Priest, presently in St. Rita's Parish, here in town. I grew up in Milan, Italy, attending a Jesuit Seminary and eventually studying at the Gregorian Institute in Rome. In Yr-18 I published an article entitled "Relating the Catholic Church to the Real World of God" in the Catholic Journal.

> In Yr-17 I was transferred to the United States, where I moved from parish to parish until transferred to St. Rita's in Yr-10. In addition to directing church, my primary responsibilities since being in the United States have been teaching. I presently teach in the primary and secondary schools run by St. Rita's. I teach Latin and several religion courses. Since being in the United States I have taken 2 courses in psychology and one course in counseling. I confirmed Ellen and Richard and baptized Allen.

> I am a firm follower of the Catholic Church's position concerning sex outside of marriage. It is contrary to the teachings of the Scriptures and the 1975 Vatican Declaration on Sexual Ethics. My years of experience indicate such activity drives people away from the Church and a life with God. I have noticed this with Allen and Ellen. Since Gina divorced Paul, the children have attended mass and communion less frequently.

> I was consulted by Paul Donato concerning the children several months ago. I

urged him to seek custody of his children. Placement of the children with Paul would enhance their moral and religious interests in addition to their general welfare.

I have visited Paul's apartment on several occasions. It is a small, but clean, two bedroom apartment located over a tavern. I am somewhat concerned that it is located over the tavern since it can be noisy at night, but it is a safe and friendly neighborhood.

For Paul, conduct an examination of Father Lonagoni, qualifying him as an expert and eliciting appropriate testimony. For Gina, oppose the testimony of Father Lonagoni.

CHAPTER 6

AUTHENTICATION

6.1 In a breach of contract action, plaintiff claims that a written contract was executed. Which if any of the following is a permissible means to authenticate the document plaintiff claims is the contract?

.01 Plaintiff seeks to introduce the document by testifying that he saw defendant sign this document and that this is the contract.

.02 Plaintiff seeks to introduce the document by testifying that he has dealt with defendant for six years, that they have corresponded regularly during that period, and have entered into six written contracts. Each of the contracts, including the one in this litigation, were negotiated by phone with documents exchanged by mail. Further, plaintiff will testify, that although he has never personally met the defendant prior to bringing this lawsuit, he recognizes the signature on the document in question as that of the defendant.

.03 Plaintiff will testify that he has never had a contract with the defendant before the present contract. He knows that the signature is defendant's, however, because he has compared the signature on the contract with defendant's signature on the deposition taken in this action.

.04 Assume the defendant claims that he never signed the contract and that the document plaintiff is seeking to introduce contains his forged signature. What standard should the judge use to determine the admissibility of the document?

6.2 **Witness Examination.** *State v. Duffy.* Assume Arlo signed the statement he made after his arrest. The statement, however, was not notarized. Officer Gorham is unavailable at trial. Authenticate Arlo's statement, questioning any witnesses of your choice.

6.3 Harold and Maude, husband and wife, are itinerant mattress cleaners. Maude, believing Harold is having an affair brings an alienation of affections action against Sylvia. At trial, Maude seeks to testify that while doing the laundry she found a note from Sylvia to Harold, signed by Sylvia. The note said, "I love you Harold. Why won't you dump Maude?" The letter itself was destroyed when Maude, in a rage over finding it, tore it up and tossed it out the window. Sylvia's attorney objects to Maude's testimony based on lack of authentication of the letter. Must the letter be authenticated, and if so what possible ways are there to do it?

6.4 Witness Examination. *Donato v. Donato.* You represent Paul Donato. Paul has an answering machine. After filing the custody suit, Paul came home and the following, and nothing else, was recorded on the machine:

> "Why don't you give up, you're going to lose the kids one way or the other."

The recording has been erased. Paul is convinced the caller was Gina. Prepare the direct examination of Paul to introduce this statement into evidence.

6.5   Assume that in the previous problem, Paul is convinced that the caller was Sam. Which if any of the following is a permissible means to authenticate the recorded message?

.01   Paul will testify that he has known Sam for several years. They coached together for many years in the basketball program at the local Catholic Church. He estimates they have talked on the phone at least 100 times, and well over that number of times in person.

.02   Paul will testify that he has never met Sam personally, but that on at least six occasions when he called Gina's house to talk about visitation with the kids, a male voice sounding just like the voice on the answering machine answered, saying, "Sam here."

.03   Paul will testify that he has never had contact with the defendant Sam before the present action. He knows that the voice was Sam's, however, because he has heard Sam talking to Gina in the courthouse hallway and recognized the voice as the same one on the answering machine.

6.6   An action was brought to denaturalize the defendant for failure to disclose membership in a Ukrainian Nazi police organization during World War II. In order to prove membership in the organization, the government seeks to introduce two documents which it purports were 1) an application for insurance filled out at the time the defendant joined the organization, and 2) a form used when membership in the organization was ended. The documents were obtained from the Russian government and were certified by a Russian official authorized to release the documents to foreign governments. Both documents contained the defendant's name. The government called two witnesses to authenticate the documents. The first, an expert on the holocaust testified that he had seen documents such as these before, and that these were very similar in appearance. A second witness, an expert on written documents, testified that in his opinion, the documents had been executed no later than the dates contained on the documents. Should the trial court allow the introduction of the documents? Why or why not?

6.7   A husband and wife are on trial for selling heroin. The government alleges that the defendants sold the drugs to a police informant. There is testimony that the informant met the defendants in the back of a van where the sale took place. The informant left the van, got into his car and then drove to the police station and turned the drugs over to the police. Having received a signal from the informant upon leaving the van, the police followed the van and arrested the husband and wife when they returned to their home. While the van was under surveillance during the sale, the police did not actually see the sale. The informant died between the day of arrest and trial. Defendants oppose the admission of the heroin. What result?

6.8   **Fact Investigation/Deposition.** Plaintiff went to the corner deli and bought a jar of "Mrs. White's" pickled watermelon. Plaintiff alleges she was injured when she ate glass contained in the jar. The jar has a label printed with "Mrs. White's Co." in bold print and "Hand Packaged by Mrs. White's Co." in smaller print. The jar has Owens Glass Co.'s logo stamped on it. Plaintiff sues the owner of the deli and Mrs. White's. Mrs. White's denies that this is one of its jars of watermelon.

.01   Assume the Federal Rules of Evidence and the Federal Rules of Civil Procedure *do not* apply. Develop a fact investigation plan which will provide you with enough additional evidence to authenticate the jar and its label. Identify the key legal or factual propositions crucial for you to authenticate the evidence. Itemize the specific evidence from witnesses, as well as demonstrative and physical evidence, you expect to gather. Finally, indicate where and how you should look for this evidence. **Be sure to fill out the joint questionnaire following development of the fact investigation plan.**

.02   What difference would it make if the Federal Rules of Evidence and Civil Procedure apply?

6.9   In which, if any, of the following questions has the evidence been properly authenticated? What additional information you would like to have before admitting the item into evidence?

.01   An undercover police officer would like to testify that he received a call from the defendant. He, however, did not recognize the voice. The substance of the conversation was an arrangement to purchase drugs. Pursuant to the telephone conversation, the police officer went to an address looking for someone wearing a trench coat. At that address, the defendant approached him and sold him drugs.

.02   In a criminal prosecution, defendant is alleged to have murdered his girl friend and then to have attempted suicide. The prosecutor seeks to introduce a series of five typewritten notes found lying near the victim and defendant. The first note refers to personal problems the defendant is having, says the victim is the cause of these problems, that she would pay, and that the end was near for them both. The note then made provision for the distribution of the defendant's estate. The second note says that a third party, "Arthur," was the cause of the defendant's problems. The fourth note was a love letter purportedly from Arthur to the victim. The fifth note, found in defendant's clothing asks the finder to notify defendant's family of his death.

.03   In an action for failure to pay income tax, the government seeks to introduce a certified computer printout of its records showing that it has no record of defendant ever filing an income tax return.

.04   In order to show that fire destroyed a courthouse in the city of Columbia 60 years ago, the proponent seeks to introduce a newspaper dated 60 years ago, with "The Columbia Times-Dispatch" printed on its masthead. The newspaper contains an article that says the police chief reported the destruction of the courthouse. Regardless whether it is authentic, should the newspaper be excluded because it is hearsay?

.05   ***Donato v. Donato.*** Mrs. Donato seeks to introduce certified copies of reports from the city Department of Licensing and Inspections. The reports were the result of an inspection occasioned by the structural damage caused in the storm.

.06   Criminal prosecution is brought against a corporation for allegedly paying illegal bribes to an official of a foreign government. As part of its defense, the corporation seeks to introduce photocopies of relevant foreign statutes that it claims indicate the payments were fees, not bribes.

.07   In a criminal prosecution for homicide, the defendant is charged with killing his wife and two children. As part of the prosecutor's attempt to prove motive, he seeks to establish that the defendant was unfaithful to his wife. As part of that effort, the prosecutor calls a former girlfriend of the defendant's. The girlfriend will testify that she received a present of a black and red (their high school colors) negligee from the defendant the day before he married his wife. The day before the wedding, defendant, the witness will testify, came to her office, said he was getting married the next day and that he had a gift for her. When she went out to the car she found the negligee.

6.10   Drafting. As a part-time prosecutor for a small rural county, draft procedures the police department should follow upon seizing suspected drugs and sending the drugs to be analyzed at the state laboratory. The state lab is located in the capitol 250 miles away, and the procedure should be as cost effective as possible.

6.11   Re-read Federal Rule of Evidence 104(a) and (b). Authentication is a preliminary fact question to be decided by the judge. In making her decision, should the judge be able to rely on evidence that would be inadmissible under the rules of evidence? Why or why not?

CHAPTER 7

THE ORIGINAL DOCUMENT RULE

7.1   Consider:

.01   Defendant, manufacturer, is charged with sewing too many pockets on jackets, in violation of war-time conservation laws. At trial, the prosecutor offers testimony concerning the number of pockets on defendant's jackets. Defendant objects based on the original document rule, claiming the jackets themselves should be produced. Your opinion.

.02   Two parties enter into written contract. In a subsequent breach of contract action, in order to prove the terms of the contract, does the original document rule apply?

.03   Two parties enter into an oral contract. One of the parties, with the full knowledge of the other party, tape records the negotiations. In a subsequent breach of contract action, to prove the substance of the contract, must the tape recording be produced?

.04   Assume that in the previous question rather than tape recording the negotiations, one of the parties goes back to her office and prepares a memorandum of her recollections of the negotiation and the agreement reached. In the subsequent breach of contract action, to prove the substance of the contract, must the memorandum be produced?

.05   Defendant is charged with contributing to the delinquency of a minor. The prosecutor has videotapes of defendant and the minor engaged in sexual intercourse. To prove that defendant and the minor engaged in sexual intercourse, must the prosecutor introduce the videotapes?

.06   Assume that the same videotape as in the previous problem is in the possession of the prosecutor. In a prosecution for the distribution of obscene material (*i.e.*, the videotape of people engaged in sexual intercourse) does the original document rule require the production of the videotape?

.07   ***Paula v. David and PDG***. Paula claims she received a broken leg. She calls to the stand her treating physician who will testify that after reviewing X-rays, he set Paula's leg and provided follow-up treatment. Does the original document rule require the production of the hospital X-rays to prove the existence of the broken bone?

Content of document

CL - No
Fed. yes
.no.relied memory

.08 In a medical malpractice action, plaintiff claims that the defendant doctor breached the standard of care by his failure to properly read the X-ray that showed a broken leg. Does the original document rule require production of the X-ray?

.09 Refer to problem 5.10. Assuming Dr. Edmond's testimony is admitted, does the original document rule require production of the documents he relied upon?

No

.10 Buyer and seller have a dispute as to whether the purchase price of an item has been paid. Buyer has a receipt for the $100, but has left it at home. Buyer wishes to testify that he paid the final $100 installment. Seller objects based on the original document rule. What result?

Yes

.11 Assume that in the previous question the Buyer wishes to testify, "I paid the $100, in fact I have a receipt that says, 'Received $100' and is signed by Seller." Seller objects based on the original document rule. What result?

No - Stat coure
X is not
?
Demonstrative
3 a m

.12 Assume in problem 7.1.05, the prosecutor has still photographs of the defendant and the minor engaged in sexual intercourse. A police officer gets on the stand to testify that he has seen the photographs. He then begins to describe the content of the photographs. Defendant objects based on the original document rule. What result? Assume the police officer offered a print of the photograph, and defendant objected, claiming that the negatives of the print were required. What result?

.13 Defendant is charged with production and sale of counterfeit tennis shoes. The shoes allegedly say "Converse" on them, and are designed to look like Converse tennis shoes. A Converse investigator takes the stand and testifies that he was approached by defendant and offered a shoe, that he then attempts to describe. Defendant's counsel objects. Your ruling. Why?

Yes

.14 In an action for conversion of an automobile, plaintiff seeks to testify as to the serial number on the car? Does the original document rule require production of the car?

No call in court

.15 Defendant is charged with rustling cattle belonging to the Circle O Ranch. A police officer seeks to describe the brand found on the cattle in defendant's possession as being the same as the Circle O's. Does the original document rule require production of the cattle before the police officer can describe the brand?

No his testimony

.16 Refer to problem 4.40.02. Gina's attorney objects based on the original document rule. What result?

7.2 A local homeowner seeks to challenge a zoning change. State law provides that to have standing to challenge a zoning change you must be a property owner within the jurisdiction seeking to make the change. When the homeowner takes the stand to testify that he does indeed own real estate, the opponent objects based on the fact that the owner's deed is required under the original document rule. How should the judge rule?

7.3   Defendant is charged with conspiracy to commit the murder of her business partner. To prove motive, the government calls the intended victim to the stand who testifies that he and the defendant had taken out key-person life insurance policies in the amount of $50,000 in the event either of them died. Defense counsel objects based on the original document rule. What result?

7.4   In each of the following instances, what is the original document?

  .01   A local newspaper printed a story in which a reporter wrote that, in a speech at a public forum, a law student called a law professor incompetent. The law professor sues the student in a defamation action. At trial, the law professor calls a witness to testify about the student's reference to the professor as incompetent. The defendant's counsel objects on the basis of the original document rule, claiming that the professor must produce the newspaper article. What ruling? Suppose the professor sued the reporter. Would the original document rule apply? What if he sued the newspaper?

  .02   In a breach of contract action, the offer was sent by FAX machine. The acceptance was sent by mail. In order to establish the terms of the contract, what copies are required by the original document rule?

  .03   Assume in the previous problem that the offer was actually mailed to the other party, with the offeror retaining a photocopy in her files. May the offeror use the photocopy to meet the original document rule?

  .04   The suit involves a breach of contract for the sale of a home. A form contract was used, with the real estate agent filling in each of the blanks. Four photocopies of the contract were then made. These four copies, and the one filled in by the agent, were independently signed by the parties. In a suit for specific performance of the real estate contract, which of these five copies is an original? Assume the copies were not independently signed, but the first was signed and then the other four copies were made. Does this change your answer?

7.5   If under Federal Rule 1003 duplicates are as fully admissible as originals, is there any difference between an original and a duplicate?

7.6   Witness Examination. *State v. Duffy.* Assume Duffy signed his statement to the police. Officer Gorham is on the stand. The following takes place:

By the Prosecutor:

Q: After you gave the defendant his *Miranda* rights at the police station, did he talk to you?

A: Yes.

Q: What did he say?

By Defendant's Counsel: Objection, your honor, best evidence.

Q: That's quite alright, your honor, I'll rephrase the question. Officer Gorham, did the defendant sign a statement after talking to you?

A: Yes.

Q: And what did that statement say?

By Defendant's Counsel: Objection, your honor, best evidence.

What is the proper ruling on defense counsel's two objections?

7.7   The Internal Revenue Service brings suit to collect taxes. Under applicable laws, the statute of limitations bars the suit unless the taxpayer has executed a waiver extending the limitations period.

   .01   The taxpayer denies the existence of a waiver. The IRS attempts to use secondary evidence to prove the existence of a waiver signed by the taxpayer, claiming its copy of the two originals was destroyed following standard IRS procedures. May the IRS use secondary evidence? Assuming secondary evidence is permitted, what type of evidence would be admissible?

   .02   Suppose the taxpayer admits that a waiver was signed, but disputes its terms, claiming the waiver does not apply in this suit. Also, assume the taxpayer is divorced and claims that his former spouse has all his original tax records. Would this new information affect your answer in the previous problem? Is there any additional information you need?

7.8   In a breach of contract action, plaintiff seeks to introduce oral testimony concerning the contents of the contract. Plaintiff claims that his copy of the contract was destroyed in a fire and that the defendant has the only other original. Defendant objects, claiming plaintiff failed to serve a subpoena duces tecum for the contract.

.01   What standard of proof should the trial court use in determining the unavailability of the document plaintiff says was destroyed by fire?

.02   Should plaintiff be prohibited from providing oral testimony because of her failure to serve a subpoena duces tecum?

.03   Assume the defendant denies the contract was ever executed. How should the existence or non-existence of the document be determined?

.04   Assume Defendant does produce a contract, but plaintiff asserts that a material term has been changed. May plaintiff testify to her recollection as to what she claims were the terms of the contract?

7.9   Peter is the owner of several rent controlled housing units. Peter brings suit against the City Housing Authority (CHA) under 42 U.S.C. § 1983, alleging that CHA discriminates against him on the basis of race. He maintains that CHA allows lower rents to be maintained on his apartments than on the apartments of people of other races. CHA, in order to rebut Peter's claim, did a survey of 150 controlled rental units in the area contiguous to Peter's units. The survey consisted of reviewing contracts between CHA and the owners, personally interviewing one-half the owners, and on-site visits of the premises. The findings of the investigation were summarized in a document containing the name of the owner, location of the rental units, race of the owner, and rent charged for each unit. The actual notes of the investigators were routinely destroyed following compilation of the data. The summary shows that Peter receives above average rent. What grounds exist for Peter to object?

7.10   Refer to problem 5.6.01. Assume that Dr. Duke claims he read the lab report as soon as it was completed, which happened to be two days after treating Mr. Perry.

.01   Mr. Perry seeks to call a witness who will testify that the lab report was dated on the same day that Perry went to the emergency room. Dr. Duke objects based on the original document rule, claiming that the lab slip must be accounted for. What result?

.02   Assume that, without accounting for the unavailability of the lab report, Mr. Perry calls a nurse who will testify that she heard Dr. Duke tell a colleague, "Of course, the difficulty is that the lab report says the test was done on the day of Perry's injury." Defense counsel objects based on hearsay and best evidence. What result?

.03   Assume that, without accounting for the unavailability of the lab report, Mr. Perry seeks to introduce the following portion of the transcript of Dr. Duke's deposition.

Q: What date was on the lab report?

A: I'm not sure of the date, but I know it was the same day he came into the emergency room.

Defense counsel objects based on hearsay and best evidence. What result?

CHAPTER 8

REAL, ILLUSTRATIVE, EXPERIMENTAL AND SCIENTIFIC EVIDENCE

Roy Smith presply Tellers

8.1 **Witness Examination.** *State v. Duffy.* Introduce the briefcase seized at the crime scene by calling and examining any witnesses you believe necessary.

Police officer Lines of site etc

8.2 ***Paula v. David and PDG.*** Paula seeks to introduce a photograph of the intersection where the accident occurred. The photograph was taken by the police the day after the accident. The police photographer is not available. Discuss the methods available to introduce the photograph and the use to which the photograph may be put.

Mgr. Cynthia Ardor

8.3 **Witness Examination.** *State v. Duffy.* Assume the bank had a closed circuit video camera operating during the robbery. Be prepared to call and examine any witnesses you believe necessary to introduce the videotape recording showing the robbery.

Arresting officer

8.4 **Witness Examination.** Refer to 7.1.05. Introduce the videotapes in the contributing to the delinquency action by calling and examining any witnesses you believe necessary. Would the examination differ if the lawsuit involved the pornography charge in problem 7.1.06?

Video operator

8.5 **Witness Examination.** ***Paula v. David and PDG.*** Wanda will testify that just before the accident she left the Peking Restaurant, two doors down from the southeast corner of Libbie and Grove. As she left the restaurant, she turned right and walked toward her car that was parked on the street approximately 30 feet from the northeast corner of Libbie and Grove. As she approached the intersection, she stopped to wait for the light to change. As she waited, she looked up and saw David's truck traveling south on Grove. She first saw the truck as it passed the intersection of Grove and Maple. She then looked to her left and saw Paula's car traveling east on Libbie. As Paula's car entered the intersection, David's truck struck her left rear. Conduct the direct examination of Wanda eliciting this testimony and using the diagram found in Appendix C. Assume the diagram is *not* drawn to scale. Also for David, prepare to object to the use of the diagram. What difference would it make if the drawing were to scale? Could a blackboard be used? If she is allowed to use a diagram or the blackboard, should the jury be allowed to take the diagram back to the jury room when it deliberates? If the court allows use of the blackboard, how will you preserve the diagram for appeal?

8.6   In a personal injury action involving an airplane crash, plaintiff was severely injured and became a quadriplegic. Plaintiff hired a professional video photographer to produce a videotape. The videotape, 30 minutes long, shows "a day in the life" of plaintiff beginning from her waking up in the morning until she goes to sleep at night. Defense counsel objects to showing the videotape to the jury. What ruling?

8.7   *State v. Duffy.* Assume Arlo will not take the witness stand. He does, however, want the jury to see his hands and eyes. Contrary to the Sherry Van Donk's statement, Arlo's eyes are brown. Also, his left hand has a small tattoo that is not referred to in any of the witnesses' statements or testimony. The prosecutor objects. What result?

8.8   **Fact Investigation.** *State v. Duffy.* In conducting your investigation as defense counsel, Arlo has identified an eyewitness that places him in Clinton, his mother's home town, at 12:00 noon on the day of the robbery. You now want to establish that if Arlo was in Clinton at 12:00 noon, he could not have robbed the bank at 1:30 p.m. To do this you want your private investigator to determine how long it takes to drive from Arlo's mother's house to the bank. What instructions should you provide the investigator?

8.9   In a murder prosecution, the prosecutor offers expert testimony that indicated the victim died 90 minutes before the police arrived on the scene. This expert testimony is based, in part, on a comparison of the victim's body temperature and the air temperature of 45 degrees Fahrenheit. A cup of ice cream was found at the scene of a murder. Its location in relation to the body would allow the inference that the victim was eating the ice cream when he was killed. When the police arrived, the ice cream was completely melted.

      .01   To prove the time of death was later than that testified to by the prosecution's expert, defendant offers the testimony of his private investigator who will, if allowed, testify that he took the same kind and amount of ice cream to his office and it took two hours to melt. The prosecution objects. What result?

      .02   Assume that instead of having the private investigator testify, the defendant seeks to have a cup of the same kind and amount of ice cream introduced into evidence and then time how long it takes to melt in the courtroom. The prosecution objects. What result?

8.10   *Paula v. David and PDG.* Marla Graff, counsel for PDG, seeks to call as a witness an automotive engineering professor from a large state university. The professor will offer to show a computer-generated simulation of the accident in question. The professor has developed a computer program that allows him to recreate automobile accidents, including a visual representation of the accident as "seen" from various vantage points, including the drivers' seats of the vehicles involved in the accident. The professor will testify that he developed the computer program as part of his research into automotive safety. He will further state that although he has never testified at a trial, he has been using the program and various improvements in the program in consulting with auto manufacturers for the past five years. The professor, if allowed, will state that in his opinion, and as seen by his computer-generated re-enactment, David could not have caused the accident. Should the professor's testimony and computer-generated simulation be admitted into evidence?

8.11   Consider problems 5.7 and 5.8.

CHAPTER 9

RULES OF RELEVANCE

A. Subsequent Remedial Measures

9.1 In which, if any, of the following circumstances is the evidence admissible?

[handwritten: no] .01 Terrence, a tenant, slips and falls on the top two steps of a common stairway in his apartment building. Terrence sues Larry for personal injury, alleging the stairs were rotted. Two days after the accident, Larry, who admits being the landlord, replaced the rotted, now broken, stairs.

[handwritten: Yes] .02 In the same action as 9.1.01, the tenant wishes to introduce evidence that two days before the accident, the landlord replaced the bottom two steps on the staircase.

[handwritten: yes] .03 ***Paula v. David and PDG.*** To help prove damages, Paula seeks to show that PDG paid $1,500 to repair damage to its truck caused by the accident.

[handwritten: yes not 407 unless] .04 Plaintiff sues a small shop owner for a slip and fall on a sidewalk. Applicable law provides that the shop owner is liable for upkeep on the sidewalk. Plaintiff seeks to introduce evidence that two days after the accident, workers from the city repaired the sidewalk.

[handwritten: Admissible to prove ownership?] .05 In the same action as 9.1.01, Larry claims he is not liable because he does not own the building. Does this affect your answer?

[handwritten: Yes] .06 In a personal injury action, plaintiff alleges that defendant's brakes were defective. Defendant was not the owner of the car, but plaintiff alleges defendant was authorized by the owner to drive the car. Defendant denies he was driving, claiming he was the passenger and that the driver died in the accident. Plaintiff seeks to introduce evidence that defendant had the brakes on the car fixed after the accident.

9.2 ***Paula v. David and PDG.*** Paula seeks to introduce evidence that two days after the accident PDG fired David. Is this evidence admissible? *[handwritten: 407 - No No]*

73

9.3   Able, a building contractor, purchased $550,000 worth of gold tinted window glass from defendant glass manufacturer. Upon delivery and installation of the windows, it was apparent that the color of the windows was not uniform, thus creating a checkerboard appearance. Able sues the manufacturer for breach of contract. At trial, Able wishes to introduce evidence that the defendant changed its manufacturing process so that mistakes in color can not now happen. Defendant objects on the basis that this testimony concerns a subsequent remedial measure. What ruling?

9.4   In a strict liability action, plaintiff sues the manufacturer of a snow blowing machine because one year ago plaintiff's hand was severed by the machine. Plaintiff claims the machine should have been built so that the blades would automatically stop turning when the operator's hands were removed from the push handle.

.01   Plaintiff seeks to introduce evidence that following his injury the defendant changed its design so that the blades automatically stop when the operator's hands are removed from the push handle. Defendant objects. What result?

.02   Plaintiff seeks to introduce a later model snow blowing machine, built by a different manufacturer, that contains the automatic shut-down design. Defendant objects. What ruling?

.03   Assume that plaintiff purchased his snow blower three years ago. Two years ago defendant changed its design to include the automatic shut-design. Defendant objects. What ruling? Would it make a difference if the design change had been motivated by an accident similar to plaintiff's.

.04   Assume defendant countered that while such a design was feasible, any advantages in safety that were gained were offset by disadvantages of such a design. Would this affect your answers?

.05   Assume that the federal circuit in which the action is brought has adopted the position that Federal Rule 407 applies to strict products liability actions. The state in which the cause of action arose, however, does not apply its comparable rule in strict product liability actions. Which interpretation should the federal court apply?

9.5   If evidence is inadmissible as a subsequent remedial measure, should details concerning the remedial measure be discoverable?

9.6   Is not feasibility of precautionary measures an issue in all negligence actions? If so, does this exception swallow the rule?

B. Compromise and Offers To Compromise

yes Admit

9.7   ***Paula v. David and PDG***. Paula seeks to testify that immediately after the accident, David got out of his truck and said, "I'm sorry. Don't call your insurance company or anything. I'll pay to have your car fixed." David objects, citing Federal Rule of Evidence 408. What ruling?

9.8   Refer to problem 5.6.01.

.01   Perry wishes to introduce a letter from Duke's attorney to his attorney. Assume the letter contains the following statement. "As stated in our recent telephone conversation, Dr. Duke denies any negligence on his part. We certainly hope to avoid a trial, however, and are, therefore, willing to pay Mr. Perry $150,000." Defense counsel objects to the introduction of the letter. What ruling?

.02   Suppose instead the letter said, "As I stated on the phone, Dr. Duke should have read the culture within 48 hours, but that did not cause the injury. We certainly hope to avoid a trial, and are, therefore, willing to pay Mr. Perry $150,000." At trial can Perry introduce the letter to show that Dr. Duke did not read the report within 48 hours?

.03   Suppose instead the letter said, "As I said on the phone, Dr. Duke should have read the culture within 48 hours, and I agree that a jury could return one million in damages. But the fact remains that to get that you'll have to sue. We certainly hope to avoid a trial, and are, therefore, willing to pay Mr. Perry $150,000." Defense counsel objects to the introduction of the letter. What ruling?

.04   Assume that any one of the above letters was sent, and that the $150,000 was accepted by Perry. Perry, however, failed to receive the $150,000. In a suit to enforce the agreement to pay the $150,000, may Perry introduce the letter?

.05   Assume Perry has settled his lawsuit against Dr. Duke, but still has a suit pending against the hospital. Perry seeks to introduce the fact that Duke has settled. The hospital objects based on Federal Rule 408. What ruling?

.06   Assume Perry has settled his lawsuit against Dr. Duke, but still has a suit pending against the hospital. Duke testifies for Perry against the hospital at the trial. The hospital then seeks to introduce the fact that Duke has settled. Perry objects based on Federal Rule 408. What ruling?

9.9   Refer to problem 5.6.01.

   .01   Assume that Dr. Duke attended a settlement meeting with his attorney, opposing counsel, and Mr. Perry. During that meeting, Duke stated, "I did not read the lab report within 24 hours, but that did not cause the permanent damage suffered by Mr. Perry. The chain saw did that." On direct examination, Dr. Duke claims he read the report within 24 hours. In rebuttal, Perry seeks to testify to Duke's statement. Duke's attorney objects. What result?

   .02   Assume that Dr. Duke was not present at the meeting, but his lawyer made the statement, "Duke did not read the lab report within 24 hours, but that did not cause the permanent damage suffered by Mr. Perry." Compared to problem 9.9.01, what additional difficulties exist in introducing this statement?

C. Payment Of Medical And Similar Expenses

9.10   *Paula v. David and PDG.* Refer to problem 9.7. Assume, however, that David said, "Don't worry, I'll pay your medical bills." David objects, citing Federal Rule of Evidence 409. What ruling?

9.11   Parker was involved in an automobile accident, broke his leg and was required to be out of work for 9 months. At the time of the accident he was working as a deck hand on a merchant ship. During the 9 month period, Parker received maintenance payments from the ship's company pursuant to a union contract. After the 9 months Parker was able to return to work, but was ordered by his doctor to do only light work, part-time. When he went back to his employer, the employer told him to go to a company owned private hunt club and do part-time, light landscape work. During this period, he continued to receive maintenance payments consistent with part-time work. After several weeks, Parker re-injured his leg. The employer has denied continued maintenance payments claiming Parker is not covered by the seaman contract because he was not a seaman at the time of the leg re-injury. In a suit to recover, among other things, maintenance payments, Parker seeks to introduce evidence that during the first nine months he did not work, and for the several weeks he worked part-time, the company made maintenance payments. The company objects. What ruling?

D. Pleas, Plea Discussions, And Related Statements

9.12   Defendant is charged with aggravated battery, pleads guilty, and is sentenced to two years. The victim then sues the same defendant for civil assault and battery.

Yes **.01** Is the guilty plea entered in the criminal action admissible in the civil action? If so, for what purpose?

No Admissible **.02** Assume that instead of pleading guilty, the defendant pleaded *nolo contendere.* Would your answer change?

9.13 *State v. Duffy*. Assume that at the time of Arlo's arrest he was taken to the police station, given his *Miranda* warnings, but did not request an attorney.

.01 Immediately after receiving the *Miranda* warnings, assume Arlo confessed to robbing the bank and asked for help in working out a plea agreement with the prosecutor. At trial, the prosecution seeks to introduce Arlo's confession. Arlo objects citing Federal Rule 410. What result?

.02 Rather than receiving an immediate confession, assume that during questioning, one of the police officers stated, "Arlo, fess up now, and we'll see what we can do with the judge. It will probably save you five years in prison." Arlo then admitted robbing the bank. At trial, Arlo denies having robbed the bank and seeks to exclude his confession to the police. What ruling?

.03 Suppose in problem 9.13.02 the person questioning Arlo was an assistant district attorney. Would that affect your answer? What if the discussions with the district attorney came after Arlo was indicted?

E. Liability Insurance

9.14 Consider:

Yes **.01** *Paula v. David and PDG*. David, after running into Paula, got out of his truck, ran up to her and said "Don't worry, the company's insurance will cover this." Defendant objects when plaintiff seeks to testify to this statement. What ruling?

yes **.02** Plaintiff was run over by a moped driven by David. In a personal injury action, plaintiff sues Olivia, alleging she is the owner of the moped and she negligently entrusted it to David. Olivia claims she does not own the moped. Can plaintiff introduce testimony that Olivia insures the moped?

yes-bias **.03** *Paula v. David and PDG*. An insurance adjuster testifies on behalf of the defendant as to the extent of damage to plaintiff's car. Can the insurance adjuster be asked on cross-examination, "Isn't it true you work for the company insuring defendant?"

F. Habit, Routine Practice, Introduction
To Character

9.15   *Paula v. David and PDG.* Paula seeks to prove that David ran the red light at the intersection. David, in order to prove that he did not run the light seeks to introduce the following testimony. Indicate whether the following testimony is admissible.

Yes

.01   David will testify that he always stops at red lights.

No-Relovgnce

.02   David will testify that he always stops at stop signs.

Yes

.03   David will call a witness who will testify that she has known David for 20 years and that he always stops at red lights.

.04   David will call a witness who will testify that on ten separate occasions he was out in his yard working when David drove by his house and stopped at the red light on the corner.

.05   David will call ten separate witnesses who will each testify that they have ridden with David on ten separate occasions and that on the occasion they rode with him he stopped at all red lights.

Is your answer affected by whether there are eyewitnesses to the intersection collision?

9.16 Pam alleges she was injured by an allergic reaction to a Swine Flu vaccine. She sues the health center that provided the immunization. The health center defends based on a consent form signed by Pam. The health center, however, can not find a copy of the form. Because it immunized 500 people in the six day period surrounding Pam's immunization, no one at the center has any personal knowledge of Pam's immunization. The health center seeks to call its medical director to testify that it is the policy of the center that whenever Swine Flu vaccine is administered the patient is informed of the risks and signs a consent form indicating an awareness of the risk. Pam's attorney objects. What ruling?

9.17   Witness Examination. *State v. Duffy.* Priscilla Duffy takes the stand and testifies as follows:

By Defense Counsel

Q: Tell us your name.

A: Priscilla Duffy.

Q: Where do you live?

A: Elm St., Clinton, Columbia.

Q: Could you tell us what is your relationship to Arlo?

A: I'm his mother.

Q: Directing your attention to June 1, Yr-0, where were you that day?

A: At home.

Q: How do you remember?

A: I'm always at home. I broke my hip two years ago and I don't get around very well and only go someplace if someone comes to get me, like that nice man you sent.

By Prosecutor: Objection your honor. Lack of firsthand knowledge.

.01   What ruling?

Q: Did you have a visitor June 1?

A: I would think so. It was the first of the month and Arlo helps write my bills.

By Prosecutor: Objection, your honor, irrelevant.

.02   What ruling?

Q: What time did he arrive?

A: Probably around 10:30, in the morning.

By Prosecutor: Objection, your honor, irrelevant, move to strike the answer.

By Defendant's Counsel: Your honor, if I may rephrase my questions?

By the Court: Yes.

.03   Complete defense counsel's questions eliciting evidence of the times of arrival and departure of Arlo on June 1, Yr-0.

9.18   Phoebe was injured when her airplane seat belt broke on landing and she was thrown forward. Phoebe sued the manufacturer of the airplane. The manufacturer defended on the ground that the seat belt was improperly repaired by the airline, causing the belt to fray and eventually sever. In an attempt to establish this defense, the manufacturer seeks to introduce evidence that an inspection of the airline's 6 planes showed that 5 of the 6 had a total of 191 frayed seat belts. Plaintiff objects. What ruling?

9.19   In which, if any, of the following circumstances is the evidence admissible?

.01   Theft prosecution. On the issue of whether defendant robbed the particular home in question, evidence that the defendant has robbed three other homes.

.02   *Paula v. David and PDG.* Paula seeks to introduce testimony that David always carried a beer in his truck during working hours and that at some time during his shift he would drink the beer.

.03   *Paula v. David and PDG.* Paula seeks to prove that David was drunk at the time of the accident. To do so, Paula seeks to introduce evidence that David has four prior convictions for public drunkenness during the past three years.

.04   *Paula v. David and PDG.* To show that he was driving carefully at the time of the accident, David seeks to testify that he is a careful driver.

G. Character Evidence For Substantive Purposes

9.20   *Paula v. David and PDG.* Paula sues PDG on a theory of negligent entrustment.

.01   At trial Paula seeks to introduce testimony that David has the reputation within the company as being a reckless driver. Defense counsel objects. What ruling? Could Paula offer the testimony of a witness who will state that he has ridden with David on two separate occasions and that on both of those occasions David drove recklessly?

.02   Suppose Paula was killed and defendant is sued in a wrongful death action. Defendants seek to introduce testimony that Paula was a lazy individual who had lost two jobs in the last three years. Plaintiff's counsel objects. What ruling?

9.21   *Donato v. Donato.* Paul takes the stand and testifies, that

.01   Gina is an immoral woman. Gina's counsel objects. What ruling?

.02 Gina has committed adultery. Gina's counsel objects. What ruling?

9.22 In a prosecution for illegal possession of a firearm by a convicted felon, the prosecutor seeks to introduce the defendant's prior felony convictions. They consist of two armed robberies and a sodomy conviction. Defense counsel objects. What ruling?

9.23 *State v. Duffy.* Arlo calls the following witnesses to testify as indicated. Assume each witness is the first witness called by Arlo in his defense. The prosecutor objects to each. What ruling?

> .01 Arlo calls Beatrice who will testify that she believes Arlo is a truthful individual.
>
> .02 Arlo calls his mother who will testify that in his entire life Arlo has never stolen anything.
>
> .03 Arlo calls a person he met after his arrest who will testify that, in his opinion, Arlo is a law abiding person.
>
> .04 Arlo calls his neighbor for the past two years who will testify that in his opinion Arlo is a law abiding person.
>
> .05 Arlo himself takes the stand and testifies, "I'm just not the kind of guy who would rob a bank."

9.24 In criminal prosecution for income tax evasion, David Daniels, defendant, calls to the stand a witness who will testify as follows. For each of the following objections, indicate whether the court ruled appropriately.

> Q: Do you know the defendant?
>
> A: Yes.
>
> Q: How long have you known him?
>
> A: Four years.
>
> Q: In what settings have you known the defendant?
>
> A: We work together.
>
> Q: Have you had any opportunity to observe his truthfulness?

> A: Plenty of times.

> Q: Could you tell us about those times?

.01   By the Prosecutor: Objection, your honor.

> By the Court: Sustained.

> Q: Do you have an opinion of Mr. Daniel's truthfulness?

> A: Yes.

> Q: What is that opinion?

> A: He is a truthful person.

On cross-examination the prosecutor asks:

> Q: Did you know the defendant was arrested for perjury three years ago?

.02   By Defense Counsel: Objection.

> By the Court: Overruled, you may answer.

> A: No.

> Q: Have you heard the defendant was convicted of armed robbery just last year?

.03   By Defense Counsel: Objection.

> By the Court: Sustained.

After the defense rests, the prosecutor in rebuttal calls to the stand a co-worker of the defendant. The prosecutor, after laying a foundation that indicates the witness works with the defendant asks:

> Q: Have you and other workers ever discussed the defendant's truthfulness?

> A: Oh, yes, on numerous occasions.

> Q: What have they said?

.04   By Defense Counsel: Objection, hearsay and improper character evidence.

By the Court: Sustained.

Q: Have you and the other workers ever discussed the defendant's truthfulness?

A: Again, many times.

Q: Do you know defendant's reputation at work for truthfulness?

A: Certainly.

Q: What is that reputation?

.05   By Defense Counsel: Objection.

By the Court: Sustained.

Q: Do you have an opinion as to the defendant's truthfulness?

A: Yes.

Q: What is that opinion?

.06   By Defense Counsel: Objection.

By the Court: Overruled.

Q: You may answer.

A: He's a liar.

9.25   Defendant, Alice, is charged with assault with intent to commit murder in the shooting of her former boyfriend Arnold. Alice claims self-defense. Which, if any, of the following evidence is admissible?

404(b) (N) - unless motive

.01   The prosecutor, in her case-in-chief, seeks to introduce evidence that Alice's reputation is that she is a violent person.

No
donelut **.02**   The prosecutor, in her case-in-chief, seeks to introduce evidence that Arnold's reputation is that he is a peaceful person.

Yes   **.03**   Alice seeks to testify that Arnold is an aggressive and violent person.

.04   Alice is the only witness for the defense. She testifies that she shot Arnold when he attacked her after breaking into her apartment in a fit of rage over their recent separation. May the prosecutor in rebuttal call a long time friend of Arnold's who will testify that Arnold was a peaceful person?

.05   Alice seeks to testify that two years ago Arnold assaulted a police officer.

.06   Alice seeks to testify that twice in the past year Arnold has assaulted her.

.07   Would your answer to any of these questions change if Arnold had died?

9.26   Defendant is on trial for possession with intent to distribute cocaine. Pursuant to a lawful search, the police discovered in a bedroom in defendant's house a significant amount of cocaine along with related paraphernalia and money. Defendant denies any knowledge of the drugs, claiming that a friend was staying with him and using that particular bedroom. The prosecutor seeks to introduce the following testimony. Is it admissible?

.01   The defendant on previous occasions was seen using cocaine.

.02   Three weeks before the search, defendant sold cocaine to an undercover police officer at a night club.

.03   Two hours before the search, defendant sold cocaine to an undercover policeman in defendant's kitchen.

9.27   In which of the following circumstances is evidence of the crime or act admissible?

.01   *State v. Duffy.* Arlo defends on the basis that he was under hypnotic suggestion to rob the bank. The prosecutor seeks to introduce a prior felony conviction of Arlo for armed robbery of a bank.

.02   *State v. Duffy.* Assume Arlo was arrested a few minutes after the robbery of the bank. The prosecutor wishes to introduce testimony of the arresting officer that when Arlo was arrested he was driving a stolen car.

.03   *State v. Duffy.* Assume Arlo is arrested for robbing a second bank three weeks after robbing the First Investors Bank. The manner in which the second robbery was committed was exactly the same manner as the robbery of First Investors. May the prosecutor introduce evidence of the second bank robbery in Arlo's trial for the robbery of First Investors?

.04   *State v. Duffy.* The prosecutor seeks to introduce evidence that on the day First

Investors was robbed, Arlo also got in a fist fight with his neighbor around noon.

.05   Assuming any of the evidence in problems 9.27.01 - .04 is admissible, what should be the prosecutor's burden of persuasion in establishing the other act or crime?

.06   Assume the defendant had been acquitted of criminal liability for the crimes or acts in problems 9.27.01 - .04. Would your answer change?

H. Sex Offense Cases

9.28   Defendant is charged with rape. Pursuant to Federal Rule of Evidence 412, the court holds a hearing to determine the admissibility of the following evidence. Prepare to argue for and against its admissibility. Defendant seeks to

.01   introduce opinion testimony that the victim is unchaste.

.02   introduce reputation evidence that the victim is unchaste.

.03   cross-examine the victim regarding two other men with whom she has had sex.

.04   cross-examine the victim regarding the fact that she had sex with the defendant approximately one year before the alleged rape.

.05   cross-examine the victim regarding the fact that the victim had sex with the defendant one week before the alleged rape.

.06   have a witness other than the victim testify to the evidence contained in problems 9.28.03 - .05.

.07   Assume defendant was convicted. In a subsequent civil action involving the same incident, defendant seeks to introduce the evidence contained in problems 9.28.03 - .05. What result?

9.29   Criminal action. The prosecutor alleges the defendant and her partner conspired to extort money from the victim. Defendant is alleged to have manipulated the victim into a sexual relationship and then threatened to reveal the relationship to the victim's spouse, unless the victim paid defendant $10,000. The prosecutor seeks to introduce testimony from a third party to the effect that the defendant had a sexual relationship with another person from whom he sought to extort money.

9.30   Defendant is charged with rape of his thirteen year old niece. Defendant seeks to introduce evidence that on several prior occasions, the niece made rape charges against family members, only subsequently to withdraw the charges. The prosecutor objects under Federal Rule of Evidence 412. What ruling? Suppose in a pre-trial hearing, the court decides to allow the testimony, may the prosecutor appeal that decision immediately?

9.31   Refer to problem 4.8. The prosecutor in its case-in-chief seeks to introduce evidence that the defendant has been convicted for rape of an adult woman.

CHAPTER 10

CROSS-EXAMINATION AND IMPEACHMENT

A. Cross-Examination Generally

10.1   Plaintiff brings suit against a missile manufacturer alleging that the manufacturer negligently handled a toxic gas leak causing severe injury to several hundred people, including himself.

> **.01**   Plaintiff calls Dr. Brown who testifies that he has examined the plaintiff, and that in his opinion the plaintiff received severe injuries caused by gas leaking from defendant's plant. On cross-examination, defense counsel asks, "Isn't it true that of the 50 people you examined living in plaintiff's neighborhood, plaintiff is the only one having these symptoms?" Plaintiff's counsel objects. What ruling?

> **.02**   Defendant calls the plant manager who denies that the gas leaked, saying, "The plant is very safe." On cross-examination, plaintiff's counsel seeks to question the manager concerning other types of gas leaks that have occurred over the past five years. Defense counsel objects. What ruling?

10.2   Refer to problem 9.23. Assume that at least one of the people in the problem other than Arlo was allowed to testify. On cross-examination, the prosecutor asks one question:

> Q: Now, you weren't at the First Investors Bank during the robbery on June 1 of this year, were you?

Defense counsel objects. What ruling?

10.3   *State v. Duffy*. Assume Arlo and his girlfriend Bea are originally charged as co-conspirators in the bank robbery. Assume that the charges against Bea are ultimately dropped. Bea, however, is called by the government which requests it be allowed to use leading questions. Should the request be granted?

10.4   Reconsider problems 3.2 to 3.4.

10.5   *State v. Duffy*. The prosecutor calls Sherry Van Donk as a witness and she testifies consistently with her statement to the police. On cross-examination, Arlo's attorney establishes that Sherry has heard of Arlo before and then asks, "Isn't it true, that Arlo has a reputation as a lawful person." The prosecutor objects. What ruling? As prosecutor, would you object to this question? What are the consequences of allowing the question to be asked?

B. Who Can you Impeach?

10.6   *State v. Duffy*. Shortly after the robbery, Arlo's girlfriend, Bea, was questioned by the FBI. Bea allegedly told the FBI that on the day of the robbery Arlo asked her to "get rid of a gun." At trial the prosecutor calls Bea and begins to question her concerning her statement to the FBI. Defense counsel objects. The prosector requests a *voir dire* examination in which he attempts to show that Bea will say Arlo told her to get rid of the gun. During the *voir dire* examination, however, Bea denies Arlo told her to get rid of the gun, and denies having told the FBI that Arlo told her to do it. Assume after the *voir dire* hearing, Bea is again called by the prosecutor. May the prosecutor ask Bea, "Did Arlo ask you to get rid of a gun?" Assuming the prosecutor asks the question and Bea says no, may the prosecutor call the FBI agent to impeach her?

C. Is It Proper Subject Matter?

10.7   *Paula v. David and PDG*. Assume Wanda takes the stand and testifies to her ties in the community and to the fact that she has a family and a "loving husband." She then testifies that Paula had the green light.

> .01   On cross-examination may defense counsel, over plaintiff's objection, ask, "You are having an affair with Arnold Smith, aren't you?"

> .02   Does defense counsel need a good faith basis to ask the question in 10.7.01? Suppose the question were, "Are you having an affair with anyone?" Would defense counsel need a good faith basis to ask the question?

> .03   Assume there is no objection in 10.7.01. The witness denies the affair. Can the defendant call Arnold Smith to the stand to testify that he is having an affair with the witness?

10.8   *State v. Duffy*. Arlo's mother takes the stand and testifies that she remembers Arlo visiting her on June 1, Yr-0, because that was the day she finally received her income tax refund check.

Could the prosecutor impeach Mrs. Duffy by attempting to prove that she did not receive an income tax refund?

D. Prior Inconsistent Statements

10.9 *State v. Duffy*. Assume that on direct examination Sherry Van Donk:

.01 described the robber as 160 to 180 pounds, 5'10" tall, blue eyes, wearing blue jeans, a green T shirt, and a blue summer jacket.

.02 described the robber as 170 pounds, 5'10" tall, blue eyes, and wearing blue jeans.

.03 described the robber as 170 pounds, 5'10" tall, blue eyes, with a scar on his left hand, wearing blue jeans, a green T shirt, and a blue summer jacket.

May the defendant properly impeach Sherry using her statement to the police?

10.10 Reconsider problem 9.9.

10.11 *Paula v. David and PDG*. Assume Wanda was interviewed by an insurance company investigator six months after the accident.

.01 Wanda told the investigator that she did not remember anything, and, therefore, could not make a statement. At trial, Wanda testifies that Paula had the green light. May David impeach Wanda with her statement to the insurance investigator?

.02 Suppose instead that six months after the accident, Wanda told the investigator that the light was green for David. At trial, Wanda claims she does not remember who had the green light. May David impeach Wanda with the prior statement?

10.12 *State v. Duffy*. Arlo testifies at trial.

.01 Assume the following exchange takes place on direct:

Q: Where were you on June 1, Yr-0?

A: I went to the beach by myself.

Impeach Arlo with a prior inconsistent statement contained in his statement to Officer Gorham, first assuming that Arlo signed the statement he gave to Officer Gorham and then assuming he refused to sign the statement. Would the impeachment be different using common law rules rather than the Federal Rules? Assume Arlo denies having told the police that he was at his mother's. How would you prove up the impeaching material? Be prepared to prove up the impeaching material.

.02   Assume Arlo testifies consistently with his unsigned statement. Cross-examine Arlo using his mother's letter dated May 8, Yr-0.

10.13   In a suit over an insurance company's failure to pay a death benefit, plaintiff calls Harold Walker, long time business associate of the deceased. Walker is asked whether he ever heard the deceased mention suicide. Walker says no. Walker is not cross-examined. Two weeks later, during defendant's presentation of evidence, defense counsel calls a witness who testifies that he talked to Walker about six months ago and Walker told him that the deceased had mentioned suicide on a recent business trip. Plaintiff's counsel objects. What ruling? Suppose the trial were in California and Walker lived in New York. Would that affect your answer?

10.14   Office Practice and Procedure.   You are an associate in the litigation section of a 35 member law firm. The firm has a general practice, but leans heavily toward plaintiff's personal injury and corporate work. Your senior partner has given you responsibility for preparing a draft of part of a memorandum outlining policy on various aspects of the firm's litigation practice.

You have been instructed to draft standard procedures to be used in interviewing any witness who ultimately might prove unfavorable to the firm's position. Specifically, the partner wants to know how interviews should be conducted so as to preserve the information, communicate the information to other members of the firm working on the case, and use the results of the interview on cross-examination of the witness. Be sure to include who should do the interviews, how the interviews should be conducted, and how the interviews should be memorialized. Anticipate any difficulties you see in your recommendations.

10.15   Office Practice and Procedure.   You are an associate in the litigation section of a 35 member law firm. The firm has a general practice, though leans heavily toward plaintiff's personal injury and corporate work. Your senior partner has given you responsibility for preparing a draft of part of a memo outlining policy on various aspects of the firm's litigation practice.

You have been instructed to draft standard procedures to be used in taking the deposition of any witness you feel ultimately might prove unfavorable to the firm's position. Specifically, the partner wants to know how the deposition should be conducted so as to best use the results on cross-examination of the witness, should such a cross-examination be required. Be sure to include who should do the depositions, how the deposition should be conducted, and any standard statements or questions that might be routinely used. Anticipate any difficulties you see in your recommendations.

E. Bias, Interest, Corruption

10.16 **Witness Examination.** *State v. Duffy.* Priscilla Duffy takes the witness stand and testifies. Cross-examine her focusing on that portion of her direct examination found in 9.17.

10.17 *Donato v. Donato.* Gina calls to the witness stand the police officer who filed the reports found in problem 4.40. The officer testifies consistently with the reports.

    .01   On cross-examination, Paul's attorney asks,

> Q: You do not like Paul Donato, do you?
>
> A: No.
>
> Q: You told your partner he was a thief, didn't you?

        Gina's lawyer objects based on hearsay. What ruling?

    .02   In rebuttal, Paul calls Matthew Vitti to the stand and Vitti seeks to testify that he and Paul coached together in the same basketball league for several years. He will also testify that the police officer who wrote the reports is the president of the league. Two years ago he and Paul attempted to oust the officer from the presidency because of mismanagement. Gina's counsel objects to this testimony. What ruling?

F. Capacity

10.18 *State v. Duffy.* Assume Roy Smith takes the stand and testifies consistently with the police reports.

    .01   On cross-examination can Arlo's lawyer establish that Roy is a patient in a mental institution and has been diagnosed as paranoid?

    .02   Assume Arlo's lawyer does not cross-examine Roy. In rebuttal, may Arlo call a member of the staff of the hospital to testify that Roy is a patient there? Could the staff member testify as to Roy's diagnosis? Could Arlo introduce expert psychiatric testimony that would explicitly say that because of Roy's mental illness he is not a credible witness? Under what other circumstances might this testimony be relevant?

.03   On cross-examination can Arlo's lawyer ask if Roy wears glasses? If Roy denies wearing glasses, can Arlo introduce a testimony from a hospital aide that Roy wears glasses? Would it affect your answer if Arlo has made a specific allegation that Roy wears glasses, but left them in the hospital on the day of the robbery?

.04   Suppose Roy was in the hospital as a patient in a substance abuse program. Could Arlo bring the existence of the substance abuse out on cross-examination? Would it matter what the substance was?

.05   Reconsider problem 2.5.

G. Convictions

10.19   In a criminal prosecution for filing false income tax returns, a witness is now subject to cross-examination. Under which of the following circumstances may the witness be impeached with his criminal conviction record? Is there any additional information you would like to have? The record is as follows:

Eight year old conviction for income tax evasion (filing false return) (served two years)

Five year old conviction for burglary (served 18 months)

Three year old conviction for drunk and disorderly (fined $50)

One year old conviction for petty larceny (served 90 days)

.01   Assume the witness is a friend of the defendant who testifies that in his opinion the defendant is a lawful person.

.02   Assume the defendant is the witness and he testifies that he did not commit the crime.

.03   Assume the witness is a prosecution witness who testifies he was told by the defendant that he, the defendant, had "cheated the government."

.04   Assume that instead of a criminal prosecution, this is a civil action involving a personal injury. The witness has been called by the defendant to testify that the light was green for the defendant.

.05   Would your answer in the above situations change if any of the convictions were the result of pleas of *nolo contendere*?

.06   If any of these convictions can be used, what information concerning the convictions may the cross-examiner elicit? How would the cross-examination take place?

10.20   Defendant is on trial for grand larceny. He is alleged to have shoplifted goods valued at more than $1,000. Defendant has two prior convictions. One prior conviction is for grand larceny, a felony. The other conviction is for petty larceny. The petty larceny conviction involved stealing a sweater by going to the check out and telling the clerk that he wanted to buy the sweater, but that he needed to show it to his wife first. His wife, he said was out at the curb in the car waiting. He then left the store, never to return.

.01   Defendant filed a motion in limine seeking to have the prior conviction excluded for impeachment purposes. The judge refuses to rule on the motion. Why might the judge choose to not rule on the motion? What would the judge's ultimate decision on the admissibility of the evidence likely be?

.02   Assume the judge chooses to rule and denies defendant's motion. What must the defendant do in order to preserve his objection for appeal?

10.21   Assume in 10.19.02, that the income tax conviction was 11 years old. Under what circumstances if any would the conviction be admissible? If defendant had been pardoned for the tax evasion conviction would that change your answer? Would it change you answer if the tax evasion conviction were more recent and still subject to a pending appeal?

10.22   Defendant is charged with conspiracy to sell controlled substances. The prosecutor alleges that the defendant employed children between the ages of 12 and 14 to sell drugs on public school grounds. The prosecutor calls as a witness one of these children who testifies to the defendant's criminal activity. On cross-examination defense counsel seeks to cross-examine the witness based on a juvenile record that includes an adjudication of delinquency for auto theft, and an adjudication for conspiracy to sell drugs. The latter adjudication arose out of the witness's activities with the defendant. May defendant impeach the witness with his juvenile adjudications?

H. Bad Acts

10.23   Refer to problem 10.19.

    .01   Answer the questions again, this time, however, assume that the witness was arrested for the four criminal acts, but none of the arrests led to a conviction.

    .02   Assume that the income tax evasion arrest is 11 years old. Under what circumstances, if any, would the arrest be admissible?

10.24   In a criminal prosecution for conspiracy to distribute cocaine, defendant takes the witness stand and denies involvement in any criminal activity. Eighteen months ago the defendant was arrested for his involvement in a scheme to defraud home owners. He and a partner, Herbert, were alleged to have tried to sell driveway repaving services, take the money, and then not perform the services. These charges were ultimately dropped when one witness moved out of state and another refused to cooperate with the prosecutor.

    .01   On cross-examination, of the defendant, the prosecutor asks, "Isn't it true you were arrested last year for attempted fraud?" Defense counsel objected. The judge sustains the objection. Was the court's ruling correct? How might the prosecutor rephrase the question?

    .02   Assuming on cross-examination the defendant denies any connection with the fraud scheme, may the prosecutor call Herbert, who will testify to the defendant's involvement in the fraud scheme?

    .03   If the judge allowed questioning concerning the driveway scam, could the defendant successfully claim his privilege against self-incrimination concerning the scheme, or has he waived the privilege by taking the witness stand?

10.25   In problem 10.24, assume defendant is charged with intent to defraud, based on a scheme to sell aluminum siding. Would your answer to any of the questions change? If the judge allowed any type of questioning, could the defendant claim his privilege against self- incrimination, or has he waived the privilege by taking the witness stand?

10.26   *Donato v. Donato.* Refer to problem 10.17.02. On cross-examination Vitti is asked:

    Q: You know Sam Gordon, don't you?

    A: Yes.

Q: In fact, you met him before Gina and Paul separated, is that right?

A: Yes.

Q: You don't like him do you?

A: Well, I don't know.

Q: You've had disagreements in the past, correct?

A: Yes.

Q: In fact, two years ago you lost your temper?

A: I guess.

Q: You smashed Sam's car windshield, didn't you?

Objection. Improper specific acts.

What is the appropriate ruling on the objection?

I. Opinion or Reputation

10.27   In a criminal prosecution for tax evasion, the defendant calls as his only witness, Wally, a co-worker for the past 3 years. Wally will testify to the defendant's lawfulness.

.01   Conduct the examination for defense counsel.

.02   May the prosecutor bring in reputation or opinion evidence of Wally's untruthfulness?

.03   May the prosecutor bring in reputation or opinion evidence of Wally's unlawfulness?

.04   May the prosecutor bring in reputation or opinion evidence of the defendant's untruthfulness?

.05   May the prosecutor bring in reputation or opinion evidence of defendant's unlawfulness?

.06   Conduct the cross-examination of Wally.

J. Rehabilitation

10.28   *Paula v. David and PDG.* In Paula's case-in-chief, Wanda testifies that the light was green for Paula.

> **.01**   David calls Walter who testifies that the light was green for David. May Paula, in rebuttal, call a witness who will testify that in her opinion Wanda is a truthful person?

> **.02**   Wanda is impeached on cross-examination with a prior inconsistent statement in which she told an insurance investigator that the light was green for David. As her second witness, may Paula call a witness who will testify that in her opinion Wanda is truthful?

> **.03**   Wanda is impeached by showing she was the sister of Paula. As a second witness, may Paula call a witness who will testify that in her opinion Wanda is truthful?

K. Constitutional Implications

10.29   *State v. Duffy.* Prior to trial, as the result of a motion Arlo filed, the statement he made to Officer Gorham was suppressed as having been obtained in violation of his *Miranda* rights.

> **.01**   Assume Arlo takes the witness stand and on direct examination he states that he never owned a briefcase. On cross-examination may he be impeached with his statement to Officer Gorham?

> **.02**   Assume Arlo takes the stand, testifies consistently with his statement to Officer Gorham, except he does not mention the briefcase. On cross-examination, the following takes place:

> Q: You had a briefcase, didn't you Arlo?

> A: No.

> Q: In fact, Arlo, you'd admit, wouldn't you, that this briefcase, State's Exhibit 9, at least looks like the one you had?

> A: Like I said, I never had a briefcase.

> May Arlo now be impeached with his statement to Officer Gorham?

.03   Assume Arlo does not take the witness stand, but he does call Beatrice to testify on his behalf. Bea testifies that in all the years she has known Arlo he has never had a briefcase. May the prosecutor use Arlo's statement to Officer Gorham to attack the credibility of Bea?

CHAPTER 11

JUDICIAL NOTICE

11.1   Which of the following may be judicially noticed in a federal district court sitting in Richmond, Virginia? Would the answer be different depending on whether the suit is civil or criminal? Even if admissible in both civil and criminal cases, would the evidence be treated any differently? How would a lawyer request the court to take judicial notice of any of these items?

    .01   The Richmond Times-Dispatch is a newspaper with a statewide distribution in Virginia.

    .02   The New York Times is a newspaper with a nationwide distribution.

    .03   The 1000 block of E. Main Street is in the financial district.

    .04   The city of Battle Creek, Michigan, is the home of the W.K. Kellogg Company.

    .05   The W.K. Kellogg Company's headquarters is located on the heart of Battle Creek's downtown.

    .06   There were thirteen original colonies.

    .07   Electricity is dangerous.

    .08   Whiskey causes intoxication.

    .09   Intoxication may cause recklessness.

    .10   It is impossible to drive from Richmond, Virginia, to Washington, D.C., in 45 minutes, if you stay within the speed limit.

    .11   It is impossible to drive from Boston to Burlington, Vermont, in two hours, if you stay within the speed limit. Would it make any difference if the judge had driven from Boston to Burlington?

    .12   The telephone number of a particular business in New York City.

    .13   Cocaine is derived from coca leaves.

    .14   Asbestos causes cancer.

    .15   The speed of light and sound.

    .16   The population of New York City.

    .17   Teenagers engage in sexual intercourse and have unwanted pregnancies.

    .18   If one spouse is compelled to testify against the other spouse in a criminal action the marital relationship will be destroyed.

    .19   If one spouse chooses to testify against the other spouse in a criminal action there is no relationship left to be destroyed.

11.2   Defendant is charged with larceny of goods over $100, a felony. It is alleged he stole a stereo system from the home of Marlene. On direct, the prosecutor has Marlene identify the stereo as the one that was stolen. She then testifies that she bought it in Venezuela two weeks prior to the theft for 6,000 Bolivars. The prosecutor's only other witness is the police officer who testifies to having seized the stereo from the defendant pursuant to a lawful search of the defendant's apartment. The prosecutor then rests. Defendant takes the stand and denies having stolen the stereo. Defendant then rests. The jury returns a verdict of guilty. Defendant then moves for judgment of acquittal based on the prosecutor's failure to establish an essential element, that is, that the value of the goods was in excess of $1,000.

    .01   Assume the court grants the motion, and the government appeals. The government asks the appellate court to take judicial notice of the fact that 6,000 Bolivars was more than $1,000 at the exchange rate at the time of Marlene's purchase. What result?

    .02   Assume the court denied the motion and the defendant appeals. The defendant asks the appellate court to take judicial notice of the fact that 6,000 Bolivars was less than $1,000 at the exchange rate at the time of Marlene's purchase. What result?

    .03   Would it make a difference if the case was tried to a judge as opposed to a jury?

11.3   **Drafting Jury Instructions.** Refer to problem 11.1.10.

    .01   Assume this information concerning travel time is offered by the prosecution in a criminal action and the court takes judicial notice. Draft the jury instruction explaining to the jury the use to which it can, or must, place the information.

.02   Assume this information concerning travel time is offered by the defendant in a criminal action and the court takes judicial notice. Draft the jury instruction explaining to the jury the use to which it can, or must, place the information.

.03   Assume this information concerning travel time is offered in a civil action and the court takes judicial notice. Draft the jury instruction explaining to the jury the use to which it can, or must, place the information.

CHAPTER 12

PRIVILEGES

A. Attorney-Client

12.1   *Paula v. David and PDG.* Paula goes to see Alice Meadows, an attorney. During her meeting with Alice, Paula tells her about the accident and admits that, while she is sure she had the green light, she was going ten miles over the speed limit at the time of the accident.

> **.01**   Assume Paula went to Alice to see if Alice would represent her in a law suit against the driver of the truck. Alice explains to Paula that she will need to do some preliminary fact investigation before she can decide whether to take the case. One week later Alice tells Paula that she has decided not to take the case. In the subsequent trial, in which Paula is represented by Brewster Rawls, may defense counsel call Alice as a witness to testify that she was told by Paula that she was speeding at the time of the accident?

> **.02**   Suppose Alice was a long time family friend of Paula's and that Alice was retired. Assume Paula went to Alice, not to see if Alice would represent her, but to seek a recommendation for an attorney who would represent her. Alice recommends Brewster. May defense counsel call Alice as a witness to testify that she was told by Paula that Paula was speeding at the time of the accident?

> **.03**   May Paula be asked on cross-examination, "Were you speeding at the time of the accident?"

12.2   *State v. Duffy.* When Arlo was arrested he was taken to the station house for booking. Arlo refused to talk to the police and demanded a public defender. Arlo was then taken into a interview room and told to sit down. He was also told that a public defender would be in to see him in a few minutes. About five minutes later, Carl walked into the interview room. Arlo, seeing Carl dressed in a dark suit, exclaimed, "Finally! You got'ta help me mister, they've caught me in the bank job." Carl turns out to be the precinct captain. At trial may Carl testify that Arlo made this statement?

12.3   Criminal investigation for income tax fraud. Arnold is an attorney who specializes in federal income tax.

.01   Carl, a client of Arnold, is under investigation by a grand jury. Arnold's work for Carl has been limited to completing Carl's personal income tax return for the past three years. The grand jury has subpoenaed all records in Arnold's possession that relate to Carl's income tax obligations. Arnold asserts attorney-client privilege. What result?

.02   After years of cheating on her income tax, Angela hires Arnold to send a check to the IRS for back taxes. The theory Alice is working under is that she will pay the back taxes anonymously in the hope that if she is ever caught the penalty she will face will be reduced because she has paid the money. Can a court force Arnold to reveal Angela's identity to the IRS?

12.4   You are an assistant attorney general representing the state in a disability discrimination suit brought by Peter. Peter, who is hearing impaired, brought suit against a local school system, the state Department of Transportation, and the state Department of Education, when he was denied a school bus driver's license. The defendants have just been served with a request to produce documents concerning the Department of Transportation's policy discussions resulting in the promulgation of the regulation that prohibits issuance of a school bus license to anyone who wears a hearing aid. You have two documents in your possession. The first is a cover letter from the Department of Transportation, written in response to your request that they search for documents concerning the denial of driver's licenses. The letter says, in relevant part:

> Enclosed please find the minutes of our January Policy Committee meeting. They don't look very good. As you'll see, Dr. Able, appears to have made the only statement concerning the use of hearing aids and it doesn't look like the Committee seriously questioned the matter.

The second document states:

> The proposed regulation denying school bus licenses to those in need of hearing aids was presented. It was asked whether there was any statistical evidence that there was a greater risk of an accident if the driver needed a hearing aid. Dr. Able responded that he did not know of any, but he did recall once reading a study that hearing impaired drivers in general tend to be more cautious drivers.

Must you turn these two documents over to plaintiff's counsel?

12.5   The parents of a severely disabled student bring suit against a local school system. The parents allege the school system is failing to provide the child with an appropriate education as required by state and federal law.

.01   The parents' counsel seeks to interview the school psychologist to determine the basis for the psychologist's recommendation that the child receive a particular educational placement. The psychologist is a full-time employee of the school system. May the interview take place without the consent of opposing counsel? Would it make a difference if the psychologist were a named defendant?

.02   At trial, the psychologist is called by the school system. On cross-examination, the parents' counsel asks:

> Q: Did you have an opportunity to discuss this case with counsel for the school system?
>
> A: Yes.
>
> Q: During that conversation what reservations about the educational program did you tell him you had?

At this point counsel for the school objected. What ruling?

12.6   Opinion Letter. Refer to problem 4.31. As a result of this and other lawsuits, the hospital in which the events described took place is taking a new look at its risk management procedures. As a result, it wishes to devise an internal investigation procedure that will allow it effectively to investigate alleged actions of malpractice and take corrective actions. The hospital has asked for an opinion letter from you that outlines a procedure which will allow such an investigation to occur, minimize the likelihood that anything uncovered by the hospital would be discoverable in subsequent litigation, and maximize the likelihood that anything favorable will be admissible in subsequent litigation.

12.7   In problem 12.1.01 suppose that instead of talking to Alice, this meeting was with a paralegal in Alice's office. Could the paralegal be required to relate the statement?

12.8   *Paula v. David and PDG.* Brewster sent Paula to an economist for the purpose of questioning her so that the economist could testify at trial as to the extent of Paula's lost lifetime income. At trial, can Paula be asked what she told the economist during that interview?

12.9   *Donato v. Donato.* Assume Paul made the additional allegation that Gina abuses the children on a regular basis. During the course of his investigation, Gina's attorney becomes convinced that Paul's allegations are true. The attorney confronts Gina with the evidence, and she admits she abuses the children. Should the attorney take any action if, on examination by opposing counsel at trial, Gina denies abusive behavior? Assume the state has a statute which requires "professionals" to report child abuse to Child and Protective Services. Must the lawyer report Gina?

12.10   Defendant is charged with failure to report $10,000 cash transactions to the IRS. The prosecution asserts that the defendant, an attorney, was laundering drug money by depositing the drug money into his business account. Specifically, the defendant took $100,000 and made 12 separate deposits each totaling less than the $10,000. Federal law requires reporting to the IRS cash transactions in excess of $10,000 each. Defendant was arrested after the manager of defendant's bank reported the transactions to the IRS and FBI. The prosecutor seeks to call defendant's lawyer and ask whether it is true that the defendant had previously come to the lawyer and asked if a cash transaction involving the $100,000 could avoid being reported by the bank, if indeed, he broke up the deposits so that each totaled less than $10,000. Defendant objects based on the attorney-client privilege. What ruling? How can the judge rule on the objection without breaching the privilege?

12.11   **Office Procedure/Drafting**. Draft the cover sheet for your law office fax transmissions. What issues need to be addressed in drafting this form?

B. Physician-Patient

12.12   In which of the following circumstances could the patient, or a representative of the patient, successfully assert a privilege?

.01   ***Paula v. David and PDG.*** David seeks to introduce the testimony of Paula's physician concerning the physical condition of Paula prior to the accident.

.02   ***Paula v. David and PDG.*** David seeks to introduce the testimony of the physician to whom Brewster sent Paula for the purpose of allowing the physician to prepare to testify at trial.

.03   ***Paula v. David and PDG.*** David seeks to call and question the physician that treated Paula at the emergency room immediately following the accident. Would it affect your answer if the physician were questioned only about what he saw, not what Paula told him?

.04   ***Donato v. Donato.*** Gina seeks to have the psychiatrist who has been treating Paul testify concerning the psychotherapy that Paul has been receiving for the past three years. Suppose the witness was a psychologist, or a psychiatric social worker, would that affect your answer?

.05   ***State v. Duffy.*** The prosecutor seeks to call Arlo's family physician who will testify that the day after the robbery, Arlo came to him for treatment of a skin rash, apparently caused by a red dye covering his hands.

.06   ***Donato v. Donato.*** Assume that Paul and Gina had a fourth child, Harold, who committed suicide two years ago. Gina seeks to call the psychologist who had been treating Harold at the time of Harold's death.

C. Spousal Privileges

12.13   Defendant, Danny, is charged with conspiracy to distribute cocaine.

.01   On the day of arrest, Danny told his wife, Sarah, "We better break out the savings, I finally got caught." May Sarah be called by the prosecutor to testify that Danny made this statement? Suppose Sarah chose to testify, would your answer change? Suppose Danny and Sarah got divorced between Danny's arrest and his trial. Would the divorce affect your answer? Suppose Sarah died between the arrest and the trial. Would your answer change?

.02   While out on bail, Danny has Sarah drive him to his lawyer's office to prepare for trial. Sarah joins Danny in the attorney's office, where the defendant admits that he was involved in a plan to sell cocaine. At trial can the wife be asked about this admission? Could the lawyer be asked?

12.14   In a civil action brought by a corporation, a former employee is sued to recover improper expenditures using a company credit card. The plaintiff calls the wife of the defendant and asks, "After your husband left the company, did he continue to use the company credit card?" Defendant objects. What result?

CHAPTER 13

BURDENS OF PROOF AND PRESUMPTIONS

A. Burdens of Proof

13.1 ***Paula v. David and PDG.*** The law suit is brought in federal court, based on diversity of citizenship jurisdiction. State law requires that in any personal injury action, the party alleging injury shall have "the burden of proof on the issue of that person's lack of contributory negligence." Federal Rule of Civil Procedure 8 requires contributory negligence to be pleaded as an affirmative defense by the defendant. In light of the *Erie* doctrine, can the state law and federal rule be reconciled?

B. Civil Presumptions

13.2 ***Donato v. Donato.*** Assume that Gina's mother has changed her mind and now believes Gina's relationship with Sam Gordon is harmful to the children. Her mother, however, also believes that Paul is not a proper person to have custody of the children. She, therefore, is seeking custody. Additional legal research reveals a controlling state supreme court case that provides:

> In a custody dispute between a parent and a non-parent, the law presumes that the child's best interests will be served when in the custody of its parent.

Another controlling state supreme court case states:

> Although the presumption favoring a parent over a nonparent is a strong one, it is rebutted when certain factors are established by clear and convincing evidence. We have held such factors include: (1) parental unfitness, (2) a previous order of divestiture, (3) voluntary relinquishment, and (4) abandonment. Finally, we have recognized a fifth factor that rebuts this presumption: a finding of special facts and circumstances constituting an extraordinary reason for taking the child from its parent or parents.

Discuss the meaning and impact of the presumptions in what is now a three way custody dispute.

C. Criminal Presumptions

13.3   Assume you are a staff attorney with a state legislature's Legislative Services Office. The legislature is in session, and you have been asked to provide an opinion on the following proposed changes to the state's criminal code. Your opinion is sought both as to the legal basis for these bills, as well as a discussion of the practical consequence if these bills become law.

  .01 A senator from a rural district is concerned with a growing problem: people dumping trash on farm land and in forests. When the senator approached the local prosecutors, each indicated that it was difficult to obtain a conviction, because it is difficult to connect the suspect to the particular trash. The senator, therefore, wishes to introduce a bill that would provide:

> Any trash, litter, refuse or other discarded material found in violation of the state's litter laws and that has material containing the name or address of any person shall be presumed to have been deposited in that place by the person so indicated or the person or persons living at the address indicated therein.

Does it matter whether the litter laws involve civil or criminal penalties?

  .02 Concerned with the rise in thefts in his city, and the apparent free flow of stolen goods on the street, another senator wishes to introduce a bill that would provide:

> Any person purchasing any goods at less than 50 percent of the goods fair market value shall be presumed to have known the goods were stolen.

13.4   ***State v. Duffy.*** The second armed robbery charge on Arlo's Record of Arrest involves a robbery of a luggage store. Assume that during a proper search of Arlo's apartment, additional briefcases and pieces of luggage were found, all identified as having been taken from the luggage store that was robbed. Arlo is now on trial for armed robbery of the luggage store. The following quotations from two state supreme court cases are controlling:

> It is a general rule of the common law that the possession of goods recently stolen is *prima facie* evidence of guilt, and the burden of accounting for that possession is thrown upon the accused.

> The unexplained possession of recently stolen goods raises an inference that the possessor is the thief.

Are these statements consistent? Discuss the meaning and impact of these two cases in relation to Arlo's trial of armed robbery of the luggage store.

13.5 ***Paula v. David and PDG.*** Refer to problem 4.45. Assume that David was given a blood alcohol test immediately after the accident. The results of the test showed a blood alcohol content of .11. State law provides:

> **§ 18.2-269** In any prosecution for driving a vehicle while intoxicated the amount of alcohol in the blood of the accused as indicated by chemical analysis shall give rise to the following presumptions:
>
> (1) If there was 0.05 percent or less it shall be presumed that the accused was not under the influence of alcoholic intoxicants;
>
> (2) If there was in excess of 0.05 percent, but less than 0.10 percent, such facts shall not give rise to any presumption;
>
> (3) If there was 0.10 percent or more it shall be presumed that the accused was under the influence of alcoholic intoxicants.

Discuss the impact and meaning of this statutory provision in David's criminal trial. Assume the statute was specifically not limited to criminal prosecutions. Would the impact be any different in the civil action? Despite its specific reference to criminal actions, in the subsequent civil action, will the statutory provision play any role?

13.6 Defendants are on trial for selling marijuana to undercover police officers. The state penal code provides:

> **§ 18.2-248. Penalties for manufacture, sale, gift, distribution or possession of a controlled drug.** — It shall be unlawful for any person to manufacture, sell, give, distribute or possess with intent to manufacture, sell, give or distribute a controlled substance.
>
> (a) Any person who violates this section with respect to a controlled substance classified in Schedules I, II or III shall upon conviction be imprisoned for not less than five nor more than forty years and fined not more than twenty-five thousand dollars; and provided further, that if such person prove that he gave, distributed or possessed with intent to give or distribute marijuana or a controlled substance classified in Schedule III only as an accommodation to another individual and not with intent to profit thereby nor to induce the recipient or intended recipient of the controlled substance to use or become addicted to or dependent upon such controlled substance, he shall be guilty of a Class 1 misdemeanor.
>
> **§ 18.2-263. Unnecessary to negative exception, etc.; burden of proof of exception, etc.** — In any complaint, information, or indictment, and in any action or proceeding brought for the enforcement of any provision of this article

> or of The Drug Control Act, it shall not be necessary to negative any exception, excuse, proviso, or exemption contained in this article or in The Drug Control Act, and the burden of proof of any such exception, excuse, proviso, or exemption shall be upon the defendant.

Defendants contend that the sale of marijuana was an accommodation. He further contends that sale as an accommodation is a lesser included offense of a sale of marijuana for profit. What is the practical impact of the success or failure of defendant's argument that sale as an accommodation is a lesser included offense?

CHAPTER 14

INTEGRATION AND REVIEW

14.1   Defendant, a well known sports personality, is on trial for murder. When the police came to arrest him, he tried to escape. His escape attempt was broadcast and simultaneously videotaped by a local television station. The camera team was located in a helicopter. The prosecution calls the television station employee who did the actual videotaping and asks the employee to describe what he saw on the day of the attempted escape. Defense counsel objects. What ruling?

14.2   Refer to problem 9.26. The prosecutor seeks to introduce a safety deposit box key registered to the defendant that was found in the search of the bedroom. Defendant objects. What ruling?

14.3   The prosecutor seeks to introduce a weapon found two blocks from the scene of the crime. The officer who found the weapon will testify that he was doing a routine search following the killing when he picked up the gun. He knows that it is the same gun he seized because he scratched his initials in the handle. Defendant objects. What ruling?

4.4   On direct examination the witness is asked to describe the type of car he saw driving away from the scene of a drive-by shooting. The witness says that he is having a hard time remembering. Counsel asks, "Was it a domestic car?" Defense counsel objects. What ruling?

14.5   Is the following evidence hearsay? If it is hearsay, is it admissible anyway? Unless the declarant is identified as P (plaintiff/prosecutor) or D (defendant), assume he or she is not a party.

   .01 To prove that X has heard of the University of Richmond, testimony by Y that X said, "I intend to enroll in the University of Richmond Law School next Fall."

   .02 To prove that X was a student at the University of Richmond in September, 1995, P calls a witness who will testify that he saw a letter addressed to X on University letterhead that said, "we are happy to inform you that you have been accepted into the entering class beginning in August, 1995."

   .03 Same issue as previous problem. The witness attempts to testify that on April 30, 1995, X said, "I'm going to the University of Richmond in the Fall."

.04   Same issue as previous problem. The witness attempts to testify that on May 1, 1995, X said, "I was accepted at the University of Richmond yesterday."

.05   To prove that X was not a student at the University of Richmond, Y's testimony that he received a letter from the University registrar that said X was not a student.

.06.   To prove T lacked the ability to make a will, testimony of Y that on several occasions, T said, "I'm Bill Clinton."

.07   In criminal action, to prove that the assailant was D, testimony by a police officer that while viewing a line-up, the victim pointed to D and began to cry.

.08   To prove that D had a motive to rob a bank, testimony by X that he heard Y say to D, "I need the money, or there will be serious consequences."

.09   To establish the identity of the bank robber, the prosecution offers a videotape of the robbery taken by a bank camera.

.10   To prove that D committed armed robbery, X, a police officer, will testify that two days after the robbery, he interviewed a bystander who said that he saw D run out of the bank.

.11   To prove that D committed armed robbery, X, a police officer, seeks to read from notes that he took while interviewing a bystander who said that he saw D run out of the bank.

.12   In a negligence action, P, a carnival patron is injured on a ride when the floor collapses. W testifies that just before the accident, X, a ride operator, told D, the ride owner, "Your floor boards are rotted and will break soon."

.13   In the previous problem, X testifies that just before the accident, he told D, "Your floor boards are rotted and are close to breaking."

.14   To prove the time of day that an accident occurred, X will testify that she knew it was 10:00 a.m., because she had just looked at her watch.

.15   Two defendants, D1 and D2, are on trial for conspiracy to commit armed robbery of a liquor store and with the actual armed robbery. X, a police officer, will testify that after D1 was arrested, D1 said that D2 told him that he (D2) had committed the robbery.

.16   P v. D. To prove that A was an agent of D, P offers testimony of W that A said, "I am an agent of D."

.17   To prove that D murdered the night manager of the Lakeside Bowling Alley, the prosecution seeks to introduce testimony that at the time of his arrest, D had in his possession a score card printed with the logo from the Lakeside Bowling Alley.

.18   On the issue of whether a P had an infection, D calls a nurse, N, who will testify that the doctor gave antibiotics to P.

.19   Same issue as previous problem. N seeks to testify that she heard the doctor, M, say to P, "I'm sorry to tell you the test results were positive."

.20   Same issue as previous problem. The doctor, M, seeks to testify, "After reviewing the results of the lab report and after hearing from Dr. Smith about his conclusion that P had an infection, I arrived at the same conclusion."

.21   Negligence action arising from car/truck collision. To establish that P suffered damages in an automobile accident, P testifies that as he lay pinned under his car, he told a rescue worker, "Please help, my leg hurts."

.22   Same case as previous problem. X testifies that as he began to treat Y, a passenger in the car, Y said, "No, go help P, the truck hit his side of the car."

.23 - .25   Plaintiff v. The University of Richmond. The University of Richmond is the only named defendant in a lawsuit. The University is being sued under federal law for failure to provide a reasonable accommodation to a student with a disability. Plaintiff alleges she has a learning disability and requires double time on exams. The Associate Dean refused to allow the exam accommodation.

    .23   Plaintiff seeks to testify that the Associate Dean of the Law School said to the plaintiff, "I'm sorry, if it were up to me, I would provide the accommodation. Unfortunately, it's up to the Vice President for Student Affairs."

    .24   When she originally sought the accommodation, the Associate Dean requested documentation of the disability from a qualified expert. Plaintiff had her educational diagnostician (an appropriate expert) write a letter to the Associate Dean that said, "Plaintiff requires extra time on exams as a result of a learning disability." Plaintiff, while she is on the stand, seeks to introduce this letter from her educational diagnostician.

    .25   Plaintiff calls Wanda, a fellow law student who, if allowed, will testify that during the evidence midterm, she heard Plaintiff say to herself, "It just takes me so long to read this."

.26 - .33   Defendant is charged with the drive by shooting of Victor. It is alleged that defendant and Victor were members of rival gangs. The prosecutor alleges that Victor and the defendant were personal enemies as the result of an altercation that occurred at Monroe High School between gang members. As a result of the altercation, a member of the defendant's gang was killed. It is alleged that Danny participated in the killing. Danny himself was recently killed in a liquor store robbery.

.26   The prosecutor calls Walter. Walter is presently in the county jail serving a two month sentence for shoplifting. Walter will testify, if allowed, that his cell mate, Danny told him (Walter) that he (Danny) and defendant, "off'ed Victor in retaliation for Victor having killed a mutual friend."

.27   Walter will also testify, if allowed, that Danny told him that as defendant pulled the trigger, Danny said, "That's for Mark."

.28   The defendant calls to the stand a witness who will testify that defendant's reputation in the community in which he lives is that he is non-violent.

.29   To prove that defendant was not in town on the day of the shooting (August 24), defendant calls a neighbor of defendant who will testify that he saw a letter addressed to defendant on Boy Scouts of America letterhead. Part of the letter said, "The International Travel Committee is pleased to announce that your application to travel to Germany August 23-27 has been accepted."

.30   At the time of the shooting, Defendant worked part-time in a grocery store. To prove Defendant was not in town on the day in question, defense counsel calls the grocery store owner, who will bring with him time sheets that show that Defendant did not work on the day of the shooting.

.31   To establish that Victor was a student at Monroe High School, the prosecutor calls a police officer to the stand to introduce a document that is purportedly Victor's report card from Monroe High School. The report card was found on Victor's body.

.32   Wanda will, if allowed, testify that two days after the shooting she went to the police and told the police that she saw defendant pull the trigger.

.33   The prosecutor calls a police officer to the stand to introduce a letter purportedly signed by Harold Johnson that states that the writer was standing at his window when he saw the defendant shoot Victor. Assume the letter is authenticated.

.34 - .36   Refer to problems 5.6.01 and 5.10. Perry, the plaintiff, dissatisfied with the treatment he received from Dr. Duke, and in great pain, went to a second physician, Dr. Williams. On the issue of whether Perry had an infection:

.34   Dr. Williams offers to testify that when he examined the plaintiff, Mr. Perry had inflammation, tenderness and a temperature, all symptoms of an infection.

.35   On the same issue, Perry's mother offers to testify that she told the doctor that plaintiff said, "My leg feels tender and it's swollen, we better go to a doctor."

.36   On the same issue, Perry offers to testify, "My knee was very tender."

.37   To prove the value of a company's stock on a particular day, the *Wall Street Journal* stock market listings for that day.

.38   *State v. Duffy.* To prove Duffy was the bank robber, the prosecution offers evidence that the FBI listed Duffy on its "Ten Most Wanted" list.

.39   P, a law school dean sues D for defamation. W, a witness for P testifies that D, in front of P and three trustees of the university, said, "You realize, don't you, P has been convicted of income tax evasion" In defense, D calls a witness who says that what D said was, "You realize, don't you, we are lucky that P hasn't been convicted of income tax evasion like the dean over at State U."

.40   *Paula v. David and PDG* Walter is called as a witness. Walter remembers the main facts of the accident, but is unclear about some of the details, and needs to have his memory refreshed. Plaintiff's attorney seeks to allow Walter to review a diary entry before continuing his testimony. The diary entry was written by Walter one hour after the intersection collision.

.41   Same situation as in the previous question except that Walter draws a complete blank about what happened at the time of the accident. He says he recalled it vividly at the time he wrote the diary entry. Plaintiff's attorney wants to have him read the diary entry into evidence.

.42   To prove that defendant is the father of her child, the mother offers a letter in evidence from defendant's attorney in which the attorney states that his client has admitted he is the father of the child.

.43   *Paula v. David and PDG.* Wanda testifies that Paula had the green light. On cross-examination, defense counsel offers a portion of the transcript of Wanda's deposition in which Wanda stated that David had the green light.

.44   Criminal prosecution for the theft of stereo systems from a department store warehouse. To prove the value of the stereos, the prosecutor offers a copy of the manufacturer's catalog.

.45   Keith is on trial for possession of cocaine with intent to distribute. A police officer testifies that as he was conducting a legal search of the defendant's apartment, the telephone rang. The police officer picked up the phone and the caller said: "Can I speak to Keith? Does he still have any stuff? Does he have a fifty?"

.46   Prosecution for drug trafficking. Police arrested defendant and seized a pager. The pager while in the possession of the police officer flashed the message, "Did you get the stuff?"

.47   Bank fraud. One of defendants sought to introduce his letter of resignation to the bank. The letter stated he was resigning because he disagreed with the policies and practices of the other defendants, believing them to be illegal.

.48   After viewing defendant the day of the crime, Renzy made a positive identification of defendant the next day. However, at the trial, held nine months later, Renzy made an equivocal in-court identification and testified that the man who ran by her, carrying the purse, "looked like him [pointing to the defendant]". The prosecutor then calls Officer Gaither to testify as to the out-of-court identification made by the witness, Renzy, when Gaither interviewed her the day following the commission of the crime.

.49   Refer to problem 6.5. Paul cannot identify the caller, but he does have "caller ID" on his telephone. This device flashes the telephone number of people who call. Paul's attorney seeks to have Paul testify to the number on the caller ID and then to have the court take judicial notice that the telephone number is listed to Sam.

.50   Age and sex discrimination. Plaintiff was not recalled from layoff and seeks to testify that the employer's son told her that the employer was not going to hire her back because of her age and that the men at the mill did not like having women around.

14.6   Refer to problems 14.5.23 - 14.5.25. The University calls a psychologist to testify that in his opinion, the plaintiff did not require the accommodation that was sought. Plaintiff objects. What result?

14.7   Defendant is on trial for murder of his former wife. The prosecution seeks to introduce into evidence a tape recording of a 911 call purportedly made by the victim two years before her death. During that call, the victim identified the defendant as presently beating her. For the prosecutor what possible objections must you be prepared to overcome?

14.8   To prove that a nonparty corporation had a fax machine, a plaintiff will testify that she received a fax transmission with the corporate logo on it. Defendant objects. What ruling?

14.9   **Negotiation or Motion In Limine.** *State v. Duffy.* The police have just informed the court that the May 25, letter, envelope and attached bill are lost. The police have no idea where the documents could have gone. The police have searched all known places where the evidence could have been. Preliminary negotiations took place between the prosecutor and defense counsel before it was known that the evidence was lost. The prosecutor had refused to reduce the charge to simple robbery under § 18.2-57, but did agree to recommend a minimum sentence. Arlo was considering whether to accept the offer when defense counsel was informed the documents were missing. Your instructor will assign you *one* of the following tasks. **Be sure to fill out and return the joint questionnaire after completing the session.**

>   **.01**   **Negotiation.** Defense counsel has contacted the prosecutor to continue plea discussions. Meet to continue plea discussions. Your instructor will provide you with confidential information concerning your position in this negotiation.

>   **.02**   **Negotiation.** The court has informed counsel that counsel should meet to discuss this development. The court would like counsel, if possible, to arrive at an agreement as to the admissibility of testimony concerning the lost items.

>   **.03**   **Motion in Limine.**

>>   **.01**   As defense counsel make a motion in limine on the evidentiary issues raised by this latest development.

>>   **.02**   As the prosecutor respond to defense counsel's motion.

14.10   Refer to problems 7.9 and 4.43. Is the summary report in 7.9 admissible as an official document?

14.11   Danny U. Fielding is on trial for grand larceny. Danny is charged with using a scheme, along with an accomplice Harold, in which he called Computer Machines International, Inc., (CMI), a large computer manufacturer, and pretended to represent Office Systems Incorporated (OSI), a regular customer of CMI. Using forged documentation, it is alleged that Danny placed an order for computer equipment worth $100,000 and arranged for shipment to OSI, delivery to be made on a specific date. On the delivery date, it is charged, Danny telephoned the OSI warehouse claiming to be from CMI. He told the OSI manager that a mistake had been made and that computer equipment had been improperly shipped to OSI. The prosecutor then claims Danny made arrangements to pick up the computer equipment, this time using forged documentation indicating he was a representative of CMI. The warehouse manager freely gave the equipment to Danny, knowing that he had no record of any such purchase by OSI. Harold has subsequently died in a liquor store robbery.

.01   The prosecutor calls the police officer who investigated the crime and who testifies that he found the stolen computer equipment in a warehouse. Along with the equipment he found shirts bearing a laundry mark 'DUF'. Was this testimony properly admitted?

.02   The police officer also testifies from his notes as to the serial number on each piece of equipment. Is this testimony properly admitted?

.03   The prosecution then calls Walter who testifies that, "I spoke to Harold a couple of days before the crime was suppose to have been committed and he said he was going to get some new computer equipment. Then a couple weeks later Harold told me, 'I took that equipment from CMI. Of course, Danny helped and now owns half, I guess.' " The prosecution then rested. Is this testimony properly admitted?

.04   Danny testifies in his own behalf that "I have never stolen any thing in my life." The prosecution, on cross-examination of Danny, seeks to introduce evidence of Danny's past behavior. Under what circumstances, if any, can the following information be introduced?

      A.   In Yr-4, Danny confessed to car theft. Danny confessed that he had used forged documents to obtain possession of the car. The confession, however, was inadmissible in a prosecution for that theft because he was not given a *Miranda* warning. Danny was acquitted of that charge.

      B.   In Yr-12, Danny was convicted of obtaining property under false pretenses. He was sentenced to five years in jail and served three years.

14.12   Counseling. *State v. Duffy*. You represent Arlo Duffy. You are preparing for trial and must decide whether to place Arlo on the witness stand. Counsel Arlo on whether to take the stand in his own defense. Specifically, you should:

1.   Obtain any additional information that would affect the decision on whether Arlo should take the stand;

2.   Identify the alternatives Arlo has on the issue of whether to take the stand;

3.   Discuss the consequences of each of these alternatives, including legal as well as nonlegal consequences and positive as well as negative consequences; and

4.   Provide whatever guidance and insight needed in making the decision.

Your instructor will provide the student playing Arlo with confidential information. **Be sure to fill out and return the joint questionnaire after completing the counseling session.**

14.13 **Witness Interview.** Assume the same facts as in 14.12, including any information gained during that exercise. (Your instructor will provide this information if you have not done 14.12). Arlo has suggested Beatrice Duke as a character witness on his behalf. You have arranged a meeting to interview her to decide whether to call her to testify to the good character of Arlo. Beatrice has been Arlo's on-and-off lover for the past 4 years. Two years ago they lived together. While they no longer live together, Beatrice does work at the same fast food restaurant as Arlo. Beatrice began work at the restaurant 18 months ago. Arlo has been working there for 2 ½ years. Arlo has been pressing you to call Bea as a character witness in his defense. Your instructor will provide the student playing Bea with confidential information. **Be sure to fill out and return the joint questionnaire after completing the interview session.**

14.14 Defendant is charged with possession of ephedrine with the intent to manufacture marijuana. Defendant's partner, Harold, has previously pled guilty, and has been sentenced. The prosecutor seeks to introduce videotapes of meetings at which Harold purchased ephedrine. Defendant objects. What ruling?

14.15 The City of Chicago enacted an ordinance that restricts the sale of spray paint. By limiting access to spray paint, the City hopes to decrease the amount of graffiti on public and private property. A group of hardware store owners bring suit challenging the constitutionality of the ordinance. Substantive law requires that the court determine the ordinance's impact on interstate commerce. At trial, there is an attempt to introduce the following testimony. Assuming timely objection, how should the court rule?

    .01 The city seeks to introduce photographs of painted graffiti.

    .02 Expert testimony is offered to establish the economic impact of the ordinance.

    .03 Both sides offer expert testimony on the likely deterrent effect of the ordinance.

    .04 Plaintiffs seek to testify concerning their own belief that the ordinance will have no deterrent effect.

14.16 Defendant is on trial for tax evasion and failure to file income tax returns. Defendant claims he did not intentionally break the law because he did not realize his wages were taxable. At trial, there is an attempt to introduce the following testimony. Assuming timely objection, how should the court rule?

    .01 The prosecutor seeks to introduce evidence that defendant signed settlement documents arising out of a prior dispute with the IRS in 1986. The settlement includes a statement in which the defendant forgoes a contention that his wages were not taxable.

.02   The defendant offers testimony by psychiatric expert that defendant is "credible, sincere and manifests a good faith belief" with respect to Internal Revenue Code obligations.

14.17   Plaintiff brings a civil rights action against the city and its police department. She alleges that the police conducted an illegal search of her home. Defendants file a motion in limine with respect to a press release issued by the city. The press release summarizes the results of the city's investigation of the incident giving rise to the lawsuit. The release states that the officers involved exercised poor judgment in failing to read the search warrant thoroughly, and that appropriate disciplinary action would be taken. How should the court rule on the motion to exclude this press release?

14.18   *Paula v. David and PDG.* Brewster becomes ill just before closing argument, requiring his associate to conduct the closing. During closing argument, Brewster's associate states the following:

> David is an uninterested party and don't waste a lot of sympathy thinking that I am going to be pursuing David after this trial, because you can't get blood out of a stone. I hope you give me credit with more intelligence than to pursue somebody out of whom I can obtain no damages....
>
>   ....
>
> Now, defendant's attorney has a high tolerance for pain as a result of representing people such as defendants in this case.... I do want to note something, and it is very important. PDG didn't care enough about this case to have anyone present.

Assuming timely objection to the above argument, how should the court rule?

14.19   Defendant is charged with attempting to transport $186,000 out of the country with knowledge that the funds were proceeds of illegal activity. Defendant asks the court to take judicial notice of the fact that a large percentage of dollar bills in circulation is tainted with illegal narcotics. The defendant does not direct the court to any particular study. The prosecutor objects. What ruling?

APPENDIX A

STATE V. DUFFY

POLICE OFFICERS OFFENSE REPORT
CALHOUN POLICE DEPARTMENT

Offense   Armed Robbery

Complainant   First Investors

Address   249 Main Street   **Phone**   555-3476

Type of Premises   Bank   **Reported By**   C. Dodge

Date Occurred   6/1/Yr-0   **Time Occurred**   1:30 p.m.

PROPERTY

$3250

Lost [ ] Found [ ] Stolen [ ] Evidence [X]

DETAILS OF OFFENSE

Reporting officer received call that bank robbery was in progress at First Investors Bank, Main St. Proceeded to destination. Arrived at approximately 1:40 p.m.

Upon arrival talked to manager, Cynthia Dodge, who explained perpetrator entered bank at approximately 1:30 p.m. armed with large revolver. Perpetrator ordered the two tellers to place money into a leather brief case. As he left the bank, a small explosive device went off inside the brief case, staining the money. After the device exploded, the robber abandoned the brief case and fled.

Inspection of the brief case which I recovered from a passerby, Roy Smith, who had retrieved it, revealed, concealed in a flap, two envelopes addressed to Arlo P. Duffy. One envelope was postmarked May 10, Yr - 0. The other was postmarked May 25, Yr - 0. The envelopes contained letters beginning "Dear Arlo" and were signed "Mom." The May 8 letter discussed family matters, including a recounting by the author of a family reunion held on Easter Sunday. The letter went on to complain that the cost of the reunion was too great to be paid by the author alone.

Officers Making Report

/s/   *Nancy Mundy*
        Officer Nancy Mundy

SUPPLEMENTAL OFFENSE REPORT

The May 23 letter again made reference to the Easter reunion, this time thanking the addressee for agreeing to pay certain bills. Attached to the second letter was a bill from a restaurant indicating that $579.30 was owed for services provided on Easter, Yr - 0. A total of $3250 was found in the briefcase. Briefcase, envelopes, letters and bill were placed in reporting officer's evidence locker.

The film taken with the security camera shows the robber to be someone approximately 5'9" and 160 lbs. height and weight, person appears to be a white male, but the film only shows him from the back. No gun was found in vicinity of bank. Two tellers, Sherry Van Donk and Glenda Berg were questioned. Their statements are attached. Roy Smith was also questioned. Mr. Smith Roy was walking past the bank just as the robber was running out of the bank. Smith described the robber as between 5'8" and 5'10 and about 155. He was unable to describe the robber's face since the robber was still wearing the mask.

Nancy Mundy

STATEMENT OF SHERRY VAN DONK

My name is Sherry Van Donk and I am a teller at First Investors. I've worked here for 6 months. Before that I was a teller with United Columbia Bank. I was at my window at about 1:30 when a man walked up to me and said keep quiet and give me the money. He was carrying a big gun and was wearing a ski mask over his face. I gave him the money in the till and was able to also give him the money with the exploding stain. The device, hidden in the money and placed in the case, had a timer on it. The device is designed to explode, staining the money as the robber flees.

I'm sure he was a man from the way he walked and his voice. His hands were uncovered so I know he was white, but again, with the ski mask I couldn't see his face. I did, however, see that his eyes were blue. I'm 5'4" so he must have been about 5'10", maybe 170 lbs. He was wearing blue jeans, a green T shirt and a navy blue jacket, you know the light summer jacket thing.

Sherry Van Donk

Sherry Van Donk

STATEMENT OF GLENDA BERG

My name is Glenda Berg. I am senior teller at the bank. I've worked here for 3 years. I was working in the bank when a man came in. I first noticed him as he walked in the door. I thought something was going to happen because he was carrying this hat and before I knew it he had pulled it over his head. I didn't get a real good view of his face. I guess I was kind of nervous and it was like only seconds between when I saw him come in the door and when he put the ski mask on. I immediately pressed the silent alarm and called Ms. Dodge. The man went to Sherry's window first and then came to mine. He didn't say anything, just pointed that big gun at me and I gave him what money I had. Then he turned and ran away.

He was a white guy, I'd say in his late twenties, but that's just a guess. You know his shape made him look on the young side. He was about 35 feet away when he came in the door. He was maybe 5'9" or so and 160 lbs.

There were no other customers in the bank at the time.

Glenda Berg
Glenda Berg

IN THE CIRCUIT COURT OF
CALHOUN COUNTY
STATE OF COLUMBIA

THE STATE OF COLUMBIA	)	
	)	
vs.	)	
	)	No. CR Yr-0-464
ARLO P. DUFFY,	)	
	)	**INDICTMENT**
Defendant.	)	
_____	)	

THE GRAND JURY CHARGES:

On or about the first day of June, Yr-0, in the County of Calhoun, State of Columbia, Arlo Duffy committed the crime of

Armed Robbery

in violation of Section 18.2-93 of the Columbia Criminal Code in that he entered First Investors Bank, a bank, armed, with intent to commit larceny of money, bonds, notes, or other evidence of debt therein.

A TRUE BILL

Harry Shrag,
Foreman of the Grand Jury

IN THE CIRCUIT COURT OF
CALHOUN COUNTY
STATE OF COLUMBIA

THE STATE OF COLUMBIA   )
)
           vs.   )
)   No. CR Yr-0-464
ARLO P. DUFFY,   )
)   **WARRANT FOR ARREST**
            Defendant.   )
_____)

To any authorized officer with authority and jurisdiction to execute a warrant for arrest for the offense charged below:

You are hereby commanded to arrest **Arlo P. Duffy** and bring him forthwith before the Circuit Court for the County of Calhoun, State of Columbia, to answer an indictment charging him with armed robbery of First Investors Bank, in violation of Section 18.2-93 of the Columbia Criminal Code.

_____,
CLERK

By *Alice Stone* _____
Deputy Clerk.

IN THE CIRCUIT COURT OF
CALHOUN COUNTY
STATE OF COLUMBIA

THE STATE OF COLUMBIA	)	
	)	
vs.	)	
	)	No. CR Yr-0-464
ARLO P. DUFFY,	)	
	)	**SEARCH WARRANT**
Defendant.	)	
_____	)	

To any authorized officer with authority and jurisdiction to execute a search warrant:

Affidavit having been made before me by Jeffery Gorham that he has reason to believe that in the premises known as **Meadowbrook Apartments No. 219, 1300 Sheaff Ln, in Calhoun, Columbia**, there is now being concealed certain property, namely certain clothing and weapons used in the robbery of First Investors Bank on June 1, and as the grand jury has indicted the occupant of these premises for the robbery of this bank on June 1, and as I am satisfied there is probable cause to believe that the property so described is being concealed on the premises above described,

You are hereby commanded to search the place named for the property specified, serving this warrant and making the search in the daytime, and if the property be found there to seize it, prepare a written inventory of the property seized and bring the property before me.

Dated: 6/5/Yr-0

A.L. Pickford
Circuit Court Judge

POLICE OFFICER'S ARREST REPORT
CALHOUN POLICE DEPARTMENT

ARRESTEE   Arlo Duffy   CHARGE   Armed Robbery

ADDRESS   1300 Sheaff Ln. #219   PHONE   555-3028

DATE OF ARREST   6/5/Yr-0   TIME OF ARREST   11:00 a.m.

DETAILS OF ARREST

Suspect was arrested without incident in his apartment at Meadowbrook Apartment No. 219. He was informed of his right to an attorney. Immediate search was made of the premises. Officer was unable to locate either a firearm, ski mask, or green T shirt. Two pairs of blue jeans were seized. Following the search, suspect was removed to precinct where he was again informed of his right to an attorney. Suspect initially waived that right and voluntarily made a statement. This was done in the presence of arresting officer. After initially cooperating suspect asked for an attorney, and interrogation was suspended. Suspect through his attorney has refused to sign summary of statement made before suspect made request.

Copy of summary is attached to this report.

Jeffery Gorham

WITNESS STATEMENT
CALHOUN POLICE DEPARTMENT

STATEMENT OF ARLO DUFFY

DATE   6/5/YR-0
TIME   11:30 a.m.

My name is Arlo P. Duffy. I live at Meadowbrook Apartments No. 219, 1300 Sheaff Ln, in Calhoun, Columbia. I know I have the right to an attorney, but I do not feel I need one because I am innocent. I am single, 33 years old, and have a college degree in English. I am presently employed as night manager at a local fast food restaurant, Roast Beef Delite. I have worked there for two years. Following graduation from college I was unable to get a job using my degree and therefore started working in a series of places: construction, landscaping and the like, but never held a job for more than one year. I have never served in the military.

My mother's name is Priscilla. She lives in Clinton, here in Columbia.

On June 1, I was at my mother's during the day. My father died 18 months ago and I try to get over to see mom at least twice a week. Sometimes that's hard, since she lives 60 miles away, but she gets lonely. I left about 9:00 a.m. and it took about 90 minutes to get to mom's. I stayed there until approximately 3:30 p.m. when I drove back to Calhoun. I went to my apartment, changed my clothes and was at work by 6:00 p.m. As usual, I worked until closing at midnight.

I do not own a gun. The briefcase shown to me by the officer looks like mine. It was stolen from my car on May 20, Yr-0. I think I better talk to a lawyer now, thank you.

 Arlo Duffy

Jeffery Gorham

Officer Jeffery Gorham

Note: Mr Duffy refused to sign. J.G.

Subscribed and sworn to before me this 5th day of June, Yr- 0.

 Notary Public

No. **3965**

RED BARN FOOD CONCESSION
Food for all occasions
3568 Granger
Clinton, Columbia

Date: May 5, Yr-0

To: Priscilla Duffy
125 Elm St.
Clinton, Columbia

Quantity	Service/Item	Unit Cost	Total
70	Box Lunch	7.00	490.00

Subtotal		490.00
Tax		34.30
Service		55.00
Total		579.30

THANK YOU FOR ALLOWING US TO SERVE YOU

Customer Copy

From the Desk of

Priscilla Duffy

May 8, Yr-0

Dear Arlo,

We were all very sorry you were unable to make the family reunion on Easter. We had a wonderful time, and Aunt Shirley sends her love. These get togethers do make me miss your Dad, though.

Now the only problem is to figure out how to pay for it. Do you believe it cost almost $600! Outrageous! I'm really disappointed that no one asked to help to pay, not even uncle Charlie. Well anyway, when are you coming to see me again. Its been three weeks and I do miss you.

Write! Love,

Mom

From the Desk of

Priscilla Duffy

May 23, Yr-0

Dear Arlo,

Just a note to say hi and thanks. Are you sure you can afford to pay this bill? The rest of the family should be ashamed of themselves, here you weren't even there.

Got to run, Alice and I are off to a garage sale.

Love,

Mom

ENVELOPES

222 Elm Street
Clinton, Columbia

Postmark

May 10, Yr.- 0

Arlo Duffy
1300 Sheaff Lane, Apt 219
Calhoun, Columbia

222 Elm Street
Clinton, Columbia

Postmark

May 25, Yr.- 0

Arlo Duffy
1300 Sheaff Lane, Apt 219
Calhoun, Columbia

RECORD OF ARREST
STATE POLICE
STATE OF COLUMBIA

Name: ARLO DUFFY

Date of Birth: 11/3/Yr-33

Social Security No.: 028-00-2800

Date	Address	Offense	Disposition
12/03/Yr-10		Check Forgery (Felony)	Dismissed
09/01/Yr-6		Grand Theft (Felony)	Guilty Plea to conspiracy to defraud (Misdemeanor)-- 3 months state prison.
08/24/Yr-4		Indecent Exposure	Conviction--60 days County Jail--suspended.
06/05/Yr-0		Armed Robbery	Pending
06/05/Yr-0		Armed Robbery	Pending

RELEVANT STATUTORY PROVISIONS

§ 18.2-93. Entering bank, armed, with intent to commit larceny. — If any person, armed with a deadly weapon, shall enter any banking house, in the daytime or in the nighttime, with intent to commit larceny of money, bonds, notes, or other evidence of debt therein, he shall be guilty of a Class 2 felony.

§ 18.2-10. Punishment for conviction of felony. — The authorized punishments for conviction of a felony are:

    ....

    (b) For Class 2 felonies, imprisonment for life or for any term not less than twenty years.

    ....

§ 18.2-57. Robbery, defined. — If any person takes, with the intent to deprive the owner permanently, property from the person of another, against his will, by violence or intimidation, upon conviction thereof he shall be guilty of robbery.

§ 18.2-58. Robbery, how Punished. — If any person commits robbery by the threat or presenting of firearms, or other deadly weapon or instrumentality whatsoever, he shall be guilty of a felony and shall be punished by confinement in the penitentiary for life or any term not less than five years.

§ 18.2-94. Larceny; defined. — If any person takes and carries away, with the intent to deprive the owner permanently, personal property belonging to another, without his assent, upon conviction thereof he shall be guilty of larceny.

§ 18.2-95. Grand larceny; how punished. — Any person who:

    (1) Commits larceny from the person of another of money or other thing of value of five dollars or more, or

    (2) Commits simple larceny not from the person of another of goods and chattels of the value of $200 or more shall be deemed guilty of grand larceny which shall be punishable by confinement in the penitentiary for not less than one nor more than twenty years or in the discretion of the jury, or judge sitting without a jury, be confined in jail for a period not exceeding twelve months or fined not more than $1000, either or both.

APPENDIX B

DONATO V. DONATO

This case involves a custody dispute between Gina and Paul Donato. Gina and Paul Donato were divorced three years ago. At that time, Gina received custody of the three children. The children are, Allen, 8, Ellen, 15, and Richard, 17.

In January, Yr-2, Gina enrolled in a night class at the local community college. The course, an introduction to computers, was a four week mini-course meeting four hours a week. It was taught by Sam Gordon, a full time member of the community college faculty. A friendship developed between Sam and Gina. The friendship developed to the point where they began seeing each other every evening. On September, Yr-1, Gina lost her job. She collected unemployment, but had a hard time meeting her bills. In January, Yr-0, Sam suggested he move in with Gina and they could share expenses.

Richard disagreed with his mother's living arrangements and moved out of the house and into his father's apartment. It was then that Paul learned about Sam. As a result, Paul filed suit seeking custody of all three children.

Gina believes Paul loves the children, but is irresponsible and lives in a terrible apartment. For example, on August 15, Yr-1, a Saturday, Allen and Ellen went to a ball game with Paul. They planned to spend the night with their father. Around 10:00 p.m., when Allen was in bed, Paul went downstairs to a bar. It seems that Paul's apartment, owned by Matthew Vitti, is located over the Triangle Tavern. There was a thunderstorm and the roof apparently leaked. The suspended ceiling in the room where Allen was sleeping became soaked and fell in on him, cutting his head. Ellen called emergency number 911. Paul became aware of the problem when the police arrived at the apartment. Paul took Allen to the hospital emergency room. He received three stitches and went home with Gina, whom Paul had called. Gina has since refused to let the kids spend the night with Paul.

The state Domestic Relations Code provides:

> **§ 20-107.2. Determination of Custody** — The court, in determining custody and visitation of minor children, shall consider the following:
>
> > 1. The age and physical and mental condition of the child or children;
> > 2. The age and physical and mental condition of each parent;
> > 3. The relationship existing between each parent and each child;
> > 4. The moral, intellectual, spiritual and physical needs of the child or children;

5. The role which each parent has played, and will play in the future, in the upbringing and care of the child or children;

6. Such other factors as are necessary to consider the best interests of the child or children.

§ 20-108 Presumptions -- In awarding the custody of children to either parent, the court shall give primary consideration to the welfare of the child or children, and, as between parents, there shall be no presumption or inference in favor of either.

*** *** ***

APPENDIX C

Paula v. David and Popular Dry Goods

Paula was driving her car to work two years ago. As she approached the intersection of Libbie and Grove Avenues she had a collision with David. David was driving a truck owned by his employer, Popular Dry Goods (PDG). Paula claims that she had the green light. David claims he had the green light. The accident was witnessed by two bystanders, Walter and Wanda.

Paula has retained Brewster Rawls, noted personal injury lawyer to represent her. David and PDG are represented by noted defense counsel, Marla Graff.

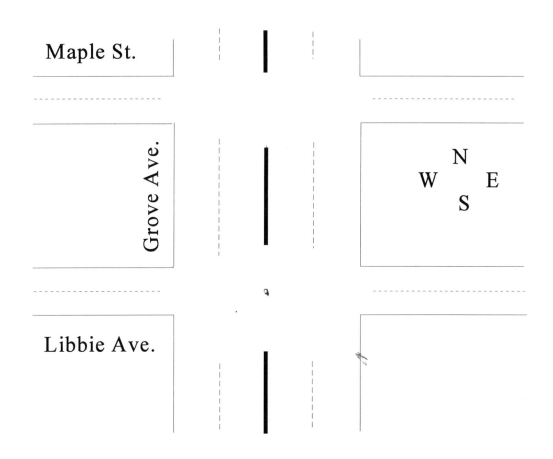